The Fragmentary Poetic

The Fragmentary Poetic

Eighteenth-Century Uses
of an Experimental Mode

Sandro Jung

Lehigh
University
Press

Bethlehem: Lehigh University Press

Associated University Presses
2010 Eastpark Boulevard
Cranbury, NJ 08512

The paper used in this publication meets the requirements of the American National Standard for Permanence of Paper for Printed Library Materials Z39.48-1984.

Library of Congress Cataloging-in-Publication Data

Jung, Sandro.
   The fragmentary poetic : eighteenth-century uses of an experimental mode / Sandro Jung
      p. cm.
   Includes bibliographical references and index.
   ISBN 978-0-9821313-3-6 (alk. paper)
1. English poetry—18th century—Hstory and criticism. 2. Experimental poetry, English—History and criticism. 3. Poetics—History—18th century. 4. Literary form—History—18th century. I. Title.
   PR551.J86 2009
   821'.509—dc22

                              2009007786

Contents

Acknowledgments

THIS BOOK IS ONE OF THE OUTCOMES OF MY RESEARCH INTO EIGH-
teenth-century poetics. The stimulating and thought-provoking works
of Marjorie Levinson, Elizabeth Wanning Harries, and John Beer provided a conceptual basis against which I could develop my own work
on the mode of the fragmentary in the poetry of the long eighteenth
century.

Among those friends and colleagues who helped me by reading drafts
of chapters or discussing ideas, Angus Ross, John Beer, Ian Campbell
Ross, Melwyn New, and Rebecca Ferguson ought to be singled out.
Elizabeth Harries and Barbara M. Benedict kindly read an early draft
of the study. Alastair Fowler—with his extensive knowledge of literary
form—gave me his valuable advice on the manuscript. I further benefited from discussions with Stewart Crehan, Heather Larmour, and
Nick Roe. To these scholars, colleagues, and friends I am immensely
grateful, as I am to the editors of *Arbeiten aus Anglistik und Amerikanistik*
and *Papers on Language and Literature* for allowing me to use material that
first appeared in the pages of their journals.

I would like to thank Lehigh University Press for accepting my
book manuscript for publication. Scott Paul Gordon has been support-
ive from the start, and I have benefited from the two readers' responses
to the initial version of my manuscript. Their comments made me re-
think some of the arguments I make and have strengthened the book as
a whole. Christine Retz, managing editor at Associated University
Presses, did an excellent job in editing my last book and has equally applied her skill and expertise to this one.

The greater part of this study was drafted while I was working at
the University of Wales, Lampeter, and I completed it at the University
of Salford. The staffs at the libraries at which I carried out my research—the Founder's and University Library at the University of
Wales, Lampeter; the British Library; the John Rylands Library of the
University of Manchester; the National Library of Scotland; and the

7

Beinecke Rare Books and Manuscript Library—were courteous and helpful, at times beyond the call of duty, for which I am grateful. I would like to thank my friends at Lampeter, especially June Aust and Jane Johns, for looking after me so well after my transplant operation, and for making my three years in Wales such a memorable and happy period of my life. At the Institute for Social, Cultural, and Policy Research at Salford, I am grateful for the support of Brian Maidment, Carson Bergstrom, and Paul Bellaby. The late Rudolf Sühnel and the late Guy Laprevotte took a keen interest in the project, and I regret that they did not live to see its publication. I dedicate this book to Paul Bellaby.

The Fragmentary Poetic

1
Fragment Modality

"The deliberate publication of a 'Fragment' would have seemed
to Pope or Johnson an intolerable liberty to take with the public;
they would no more have thought of publishing an uncompleted
poem than of publishing the first two acts of a play."

—James Sutherland,
A Preface to Eighteenth-Century Poetry

INTRODUCTION

RECENT SCHOLARSHIP ON EIGHTEENTH-CENTURY POETRY HAS MARKED
a departure from the "paradigms of the old literary history."[1] Critics
such as Paula R. Backscheider, Jennifer Keith, and Gabrielle Starr
have explored alternative canons of poetry, focusing on issues of gender
to garner an understanding of a new poetic landscape that is inclusive
and gives attention to those poems "that were not only outside the
canon but outside the concept of poetic tradition."[2] Starr's work especially occupies itself with a reconsideration of the lyric, reminding readers that "critics have sometimes overlooked what the lyric was—hymns
as well as odes, fragments embedded in longer poems as well as sonnets, drinking songs as well as ballads."[3] She explores the "seeming
generic heterodoxies" of eighteenth-century literary history and notes
that "productions from ballads to odes entered a world newly marked
by a large-scale reorganization and destabilization of literary genres."[4]
Jennifer Keith's *Poetry and the Feminine* (2005), like Backscheider's and
Starr's works, makes it possible "to render the usual trajectory from
'Augustan' to 'Romantic' obsolete" and to reinvigorate the study of form
by interpreting the use of genre (by both male and female authors) "as a
lens for revealing their distinctive achievements."[5] Renewed interest in
questions of eighteenth-century genre is also reflected, most recently, in

Bill Overton's well-informed, empirical study of form, *The Eighteenth-Century Verse Epistle* (2007). Other recent works on poetry by Dustin Griffin and Sauvir Kaul have explored ideas of nationhood and patriotism, while yet another group of scholars, including Donna Landry and William Christmas, has done ground-breaking work on laboring-class poetry.[6] These new works on eighteenth-century poetry have continued the revision of the canon initiated by Roger Lonsdale's seminal *New Oxford Book of Eighteenth-Century Verse* (1984) and *Eighteenth-Century Women Poets* (1989), as well as Eric Rothstein's insightful account of the poetry of the century. Rothstein's study has contributed to a better understanding of poetics and has made a persuasive case for reading poems by "minor" authors. His study also centrally revisits the meaning of form. He notes that "from the Restoration to about 1730, most critics practiced formalist, preceptive criticism. They tried to work toward a set of principles for each genre from the epic to the greater lyric down to the epigram, the epitaph, the song."[7] While acknowledging that early eighteenth-century critics provided descriptive poetics that were then (and in the first part of the twentieth century) largely elevated to, and interpreted as, prescriptive poetics, he does not comment on the modal associations of the fragmentary inherent in such prominent genres as the ode and the epic. Poetry in the period is, above all, a locus for generic variation and experimentation. Kinds such as the ode and the epic *are* theorized, but poetic practice often differs significantly from the ideal and, instead, reflects more directly a form's "contamination" and "destabilization" (Starr's terms) through other genres, as well as modal cooperation. One of the modes that is symbiotically linked to many genres throughout the century is the fragmentary.

The Fragmentary Poetic understands itself as a contribution to the debate about the charting of the poetic landscape of the eighteenth century and the reinterpretation of literary history, rejecting notions of poetic structure (and poetics generally) that the "old literary history"—as in the epigraph to this chapter—advocated. It aims to explore a temporal window (roughly 1690–1800) that is central to understanding the definitional and ideological differences between early eighteenth-century and Romantic poetics. This book is the first study of the fragmentary mode and its deployment in the poetry of the eighteenth century. It explores the experimental character of fragment composition, which, according to Christopher A. Strathman's *Romantic Poetry and the Fragmentary Imperative* (2006), "emerges with special clarity and force during the second half of the eighteenth century."[8] Rather than focusing on a small number of canonic authors—as previous studies of the Romantic poetic of the fragment have done—the present study's focus is on eighteenth-century poems (mostly published before 1770) by both minor and major authors who experimented with the associations and implications of the fragmentary and used it more diversely (albeit more tentatively and experimentally) than their Romantic successors.

When Howard Erskine-Hill comments that the Augustans "drew order and grace out of shifting formlessness,"[9] he may be repeating a traditional stance about eighteenth-century poetics, but he may also be referring to the endeavor of writers of the period to negotiate their anxieties in an age that was far removed from the pastoral vision of the idylls of William Shenstone or the beauties of James Thomson's *The Seasons*. It was an age of war, in which the Union of the two kingdoms was far from smooth or unproblematic; it was a climate of restlessness and fragmentation, with a pronounced longing for idyllic life, but also the recognition that the primitive harmony of rural communities, as in Oliver Goldsmith's *The Deserted Village*, was under threat. I suggest that classical perfection, in the guise of neo-classical architecture in Britain and media of visual and literary art, served as both an ideal and tangible means to counter the sense of instability that permeated society. Writers frequently voiced anxieties about personal and national identity, as well as the feared breakdown of the social order, through modes of incompleteness and ambiguity, emphasizing the fragmented and divided state of the cultural landscape of post-Union Britain.

Despite the potential insight that an examination of the fragmentary mode offers to scholars, relatively little has been published on the poetics of the fragment in the eighteenth century, a fact that can perhaps be explained by the widespread turn to historical, political, and ideological contexts rather than an engagement with poetics. The only study dedicated to the fragment in the eighteenth century is Elizabeth Wanning Harries's *The Unfinished Manner: Essays on the Fragment in the Later Eighteenth Century* (1994), which covers late eighteenth-century uses of the fragment form and focuses on prose and the representational implications of ruins. Harries does not at length discuss genre-specific questions, nor does she consider eighteenth-century poetry and its appropriation of the fragmentary. Her study is valuable, as it offers insights into the uses of the "unfinished manner" in the late eighteenth century, arguing that "the fragment offered formal strategies for dealing with the continuing questions of identity, materiality, and temporality." Rather than understanding the mode as "a sign of inadequacy"—as traditionalists like Sutherland insisted—it is a "deliberate strategy" employed by poets to deal with the fragmentariness of the human condition.[10] The intentionality that Harries stresses is equally important for my argument about the widespread use of the mode in eighteenth-century poetry: the unfinished was deliberately (and, often, skillfully) used by poets who associated the fragmentary with ideas ranging from the incomplete, the sublime, memory, the past, authenticity, and the Gothic.

Two other scholars deserve mention: Thomas McFarland and Marjorie Levinson have contributed significantly to the understanding of the fragment as a fully realized, Romantic kind. In *Romanticism and the Forms of Ruin* (1981), McFarland identifies the "diasparactive triad"—meaning "incompleteness, fragmentation, and ruin"—as a characteristic of the Romantic genre,[11] whereas Levinson develops a typology of the Romantic fragment poem (RFP) in her book of the same title. She states, however, that she has not

> in any way proved that some time between the early eighteenth century and the early nineteenth century certain widely shared assumptions about poetic closure changed, and changed so radically that poems which no rightminded editor nor poet would have 'obtruded' on the public began to appear in number and to enjoy a notable popularity. . . . There are undoubtedly examples, and important ones, of fragment publication by sixteenth-, seventeenth-, and early eighteenth-century poets and editors, as there are certainly instances of Romantic readers, editors, and poets unable to conceive the fragment as a poetic form.[12]

Unfortunately, Levinson's statement has not triggered extensive interest in researching the occurrence and generic developments of the fragment —both as a form and mode—in eighteenth-century poetry. As an exception, John Beer has highlighted the transformative character of the transitional decades of the mid-eighteenth century and traced the "roots" of the poetic fragment to the early eighteenth century and its various poetic experiments.[13] On the whole, however, critics have not further explored the hybridization of genre and its particular uses of the fragmentary in the period. In fact, the diversity of poetic deployments makes it impossible to outline a consistent typology of the mode; rather, the multivalence of the incomplete form with associations of open-endedness, a greater whole, or remnants of the past enables the fragment to become meaningful in more ways than a clearly generically defined kind can.

The advantages of modes over kinds relate to their potential to mutate, transform themselves, and enter into relationships of generic cooperation with other modes and forms. The fragmentary is a mode, like satire, that can use any genre and alter it formally and morphologically, or reflect its fragmentariness semantically and thematically. It is not recognized as a kind in the eighteenth century, for as Alastair Fowler points out, "Every kind is characterized by an *external structure*."[14] He insists that "the kinds, however elusive, objectively exist. Their boundaries may not be hard-edged, but they can nonetheless exclude. This is shown by the fact that features are often characteristic through their absence."[15] This means that, while fragment modality occurred in the eighteenth century in a variety of contexts and manifestations, it was only at the end of the century that the "external structure" of Fowler's kind became exclusive enough to be realized as a genre and that the Romantic fragment of the type that Levinson outlines was "born."[16]

DEFINING FRAGMENT MODALITY

In *The Fragment: Towards a History and Poetics of a Performative Genre* (2004), Camelia Elias notes:

> Understanding the concept of "fragment" is first and foremost a question of style. . . . The word derives from the Latin *fragmentum*, remnant, whose root, *frangere*, means to break into fragments. . . . Most definitions drawing upon the above etymology, presuppose, formally speaking, that a relation between part and whole is constitutive of the notion of the fragment. The consequence of defining the fragment in terms of a part/whole relation is that the fragment is always seen as derived from and subordinate to an original whole text.[17]

While Elias's argument about the "part/whole relation" is prominent in eighteenth-century uses of the fragment, the mode of the fragmentary is not seen as inferior to "complete" structures but as complementing other modes; in that respect, the fragmentary frequently interacts with other genres, entering into a union that highlights both the aspects of openness and those of completeness. While a purported fragment of a larger poem, such as an epic, is defined in relation to the imagined whole, it yet is read on its own terms as a complete work. Examples are Spenserian forgeries that were published as newly discovered cantos of *The Faerie Queene*. While they related to the ideological and moral framework of Spenser's work, they frequently provided narratives of their own that could be open-ended or complete. In this instance, the fragment's association with a framework of authenticity (that is, a canonic text) contextualizes the form as the product of inquiry and recovery. In other cases, fragments themselves are elevated to the status of treasures of antiquity, reflecting through their very existence the resilience of the fragmentary against dissolution and its importance as an emblem of survival. An example is Lady Elizabeth Halket Wardlaw's *Hardyknute. A Fragment.* Yet, other poems use the fragmentary to indicate the absence of context or formal structures of discontinuity that create *effects* of fragmentariness. These are skillful constructions of abruptness and spontaneity that utilize juxtapositions of, and contrasts between, rhyme and ruptured meaning. Examples of this use of the fragmentary are the ode and the long-poem, which adopt a manner of the discontinuous that I shall term "Pindaric." The ode frequently also both structurally and thematically represents the speaker's desire to move from uncertainty to certainty, from meaningless voice to inspired identity. The emblematic representation of the ruinous is another incarnation of the fragmentary, which can be rendered by means of unfinished poetry using elusive asterisks at the end of the text. Other poems describe the material ruin and convey a sense of cultural fragmentation, decline, and loss; while linking the ruin with memory, the poem's structure shapes in response to the speaker's subjective and unpremeditated psyche, a feature of Romantic fragmentary compositions such as Charlotte Smith's *Beachy Head*.

The above list of uses of the fragmentary illustrates that its associations of discontinuity, rupture, artistic activity in progress, and openness of form appealed to eighteenth-century poets. As a mode, the fragmentary "has few if any external rules, but evokes a historical kind through samples of its internal repertoire."[18] Above all, it evokes and creates contexts, if used deliberately. The "internal repertoire" of the mode can be structural and ideational; it can depend on the interaction of one mode with another, as well as on the recontextualization of extracts into frameworks of fragmentariness, completion, and closure. A mode, unlike a kind, is not confined to literary productions but can be applied in a wide variety of spheres of cultural production. Some of the explicitly titled "fragments" introduced in this study represent products whose authors responded to one or more of the generic developments that I will discuss. Furthermore, the modal qualities of the fragment are informed by generic cross-fertilization and frequently reflect formal hybridity. Finally, the fragmentary is not necessarily used only in fragments but can also be accommodated by a variety of other forms.

THE ANTHOLOGIZING IMPULSE

One major form of compositeness, planned discontinuity, and structures of fragmentation is the poetry anthology. The anthologizing mode—drawing on strategies such as the sequence—was variously deployed and developed in the eighteenth century. "Beauties" anthologies, in particular, included fragments and fragmentary compositions such as odes and songs, as well as portions of longer well-known works. While it was not the principal editorial aim to popularize the fragmentary as a (legitimate) mode of poetic expression, the selection of the most beautiful and popular passages of a longer composition indirectly helped to introduce fragmented works to the public. The poetry miscellanies that began to appear in the second half of the sixteenth century often incorporated fragment compositions, and thus turned into a significant publishing locus for poetic fragments, until the print culture of the seventeenth and eighteenth centuries revolutionized publishing and made poetic works accessible to a more diverse reading audience that no longer consisted exclusively of the privileged members of the aristocracy. In fact, collections of philosophical writings, such as those of the Earl of Shaftesbury, were characterized by the notion of the fragmentary that Oscar Kenshur has explored in *Open Form and the Shape of Ideas* (1986). Shaftesbury's *Characteristicks* represents generic fragmentariness and, through its popularity, is likely to have contributed to popularizing the mode of the fragmentary. Lawrence Klein, in a discussion of the "unusual form" of *Characteristicks*, observes that the work is "composite" "both in its contents and its form," combining "different genres and styles."[19] Klein explains that "it was not written as a whole but was in fact an anthology, representing (more or less) the complete works of Shaftesbury, gathered together and supplemented with new material."[20] It embodies the evolutionary element that Jerome McGann considers essential in the textual condition.[21]

Shorter pieces—including "designated" fragments—were published in the wide variety of anthologies, "Beauties," or miscellanies, which represented the taste of the time far more accurately than any other single poetical publication. These anthologies were important indicators of changes in taste and trends affecting the uses of form and mode. Anthologies such as *Tottel's Miscellany* (1557) included songs that quite frequently displayed the fragmentariness so typical of eighteenth-century genres like the ode. John Dryden's *Miscellany* (1684) was one of the first printed anthologies that established new standards of composition and compilation.[22] According to Barbara M. Benedict, "Collections were signs of a coterie: to be published with Pope made a poet seem comparable with Pope."[23] Benedict, however, does not consider the multigeneric makeup of some collections and the effect the various genres and modes published together had on the reader's perception; it may be suggested, in this regard, that the publication of fragments alongside canonical texts also contributed to acknowledging the fragmentary as an established mode of literary expression—at least, it facilitated its acceptance into the canon of poetic forms.

Apart from anthologies following the tradition of Dryden, "Beauties" anthologies fragmented longer works and introduced particular aspects of the author's productions to the reading public. The collection became a potpourri, a collection of flowers nicely arranged in which the editor could formulate a recontextualizing program to make it palatable and delectable to his readers. Instead of reprinting the author's entire poetic work, central parts of the production were reprinted to serve as appetizers to induce readers to "consume" the whole composition. Anthologies were published throughout the century, and found avid readers not only in the literate (male) middle classes, but among women, too. Robert Dodsley, with his pioneering anthology, *A Collection of Poems by Several Hands* (1748–58, revised and continued by Pearch in 1775), instead of publishing complete editions of poets, decided to collect popular poetry and publish only those poems that had previously been printed in magazines and journals and that had usually met with readers' approval and appreciation.[24] Far from including complete poems, however, Dodsley repeatedly uses either excerpts from, or individual parts of, popular compositions, and even encourages the publication of partial imitations of famous works; for instance, he includes "An Imitation of the Prophecy of Nerus. From Horace, Book III, Ode XXV" in the first volume of his *Collection of Poems by Several Hands*. This imitation is conceptualized as a completed production, but it nevertheless refers to a greater whole into which it has to be integrated. Notwithstanding its title reference to Horace's production, the imitation draws on Horace only generically rather than imitating or translating the original literally. Although poets attempted to copy the structure and composition, as well as the classical language, of their Latin, Greek, or Hebrew models, they ultimately failed to produce perfect imitations, since the imitation is torn out of its context and has to be reunited with the original writing to be understood properly. The fragmented text's extratextual allusiveness replicates the reconstruction and recovery process, as well as the retrieval of past completeness that fragment poems repeatedly set out to accomplish.

While Dodsley would certainly not have had the explicit intention of promoting the new (and, in many respects, revolutionary) form of the fragment, "Beauties" anthologies reproduced selections and excerpts, fragments as well as individual passages of both poetry and prose, to reflect the taste of the time.[25] One of these, *The Lady's Poetical Magazine; or, Beauties of British Poetry,* was directly aimed at a growing female readership. Its declared objective was to liberate women readers from the constraints imposed by the domination of the male readers. The "Introductory Address" by the editor states the aim of the anthology:

> Too long has Man, engrossing ev'ry art,
> Dar'd to reject the Female's rightful part;
> As if to him, alone, had been confin'd,
> Heav'n's greatest gift, a scientifick mind.[26]
>
> (1–4)

Apart from including the most beautiful parts of a variety of poems, it was essential to group these fragments in a special order not only to create a thematically coherent compilation but also to fulfill a didactic task; it was expected that by reading these fragmented compositions, women would absorb one unifying idea of (Puritan) morality, decency, and the values of a patriarchally structured society. Laurence Sterne (1712–68) was one of those sentimental writers whose works were repeatedly anthologized — *The Beauties of Sterne, including all his pathetic tales and most distinguished observations on life, selected for the heart of sensibility* (1784) reproduced sermons and, like the epistolary novels of Richardson, served as a conduct book and moral guide for young female readers. The editorial principle motivating the editor of *The Beauties of Sterne* is the promotion of "the spirit of humanity."[27] He stresses that:

> it was highly necessary on a particular score to make this selection: the chaste lovers of literature were not only deprived themselves of the pleasure and instruction so conspicuous in this magnificent assemblage of Genius, but their rising offspring, whose minds it would polish to the highest perfection were prevented from tasting the enjoyment likewise.[28]

By eliminating those parts of Sterne's work that might offend the "chaste lovers of literature," the editor not only changes the inherent structure of Sterne's work, but also creates new fragments that the reader then has to piece together to achieve the "highest perfection" that chapters such as "Compassion," "Charity," "Contentment," or "Consolation" can afford.[29] The anthologizing impulse of "Beauties" pre-empted criticism, such as that of Clara Reeve who had censured the obscene in *Tristram Shandy* as unbefitting a clergyman and inappropriate for the young and inexperienced female reader. The main choice of beauties (137 extracts) was therefore taken from the "Sermons." The extracts from the "Sermons" are not significantly altered or amended internally, yet their removal from their original context into that of the anthology does free them from the associations that dogged their original publication.

Selections from *Tristram Shandy* were treated differently. Since Sterne "emphasised the digressive, episodic and fragmentary nature of his own writings with the frequent incorporation of numerous interpolated tales and fragments,"[30] the editor had a less difficult task in choosing appropriate (meaning inoffensive) passages and episodes. At the same time, however, the compiler creates "connections" and—as Heather Larmour argues—produces "a less fragmentary representation of Sterne as a novelist."[31] Larmour has identified structural parallels in *Tristram Shandy* and the compilational structure of an anthology, for:

> the editing of the collection [*The Beauties of Sterne*] and its arrangement under alphabetical heads does much more than promote a varied and fragmentary reading experience of Sterne, comparable to that found in his own novels. Above all, the anthology removes Sterne from his writings, . . . Sterne has "disappeared from the presentation of his text" and is replaced by the characterisation represented by the anthology's titular "Sterne". Removing asides and digressions which disrupt an extract's unity and betray its removal from its original context, ensures that Sterne stands "complete" in anthologised form without the need for prior knowledge or understanding of his writings.[32]

Moderns such as Sterne or Oliver Goldsmith were not the only authors represented in "Beauties" anthologies; rather, the interest in the epic and "primitive" genius was reflected in William Holwell's *The Beauties of Homer* (1775) and William Dodd's *The Beauties of Shakespeare* (1783). The selected parts of various poetic works were assembled with a specific aim, and even poetry that on its own would have been regarded as possessing little merit was integrated in the manufactured structure of a whole in which the transitions and the fragmentation entailed in the decontextualization of the original were no longer strikingly obvious. In that sense, the various different parts made up one "new" whole. Yet this "whole," Barbara Benedict argues, "was more than the sum of the parts."[33]

ORGANICITY AND "VEGETABLE" GENIUS

While anthologies used the horticultural metaphor of an arrangement of flowers, Edward Young (bap. 1683–1765) deployed a vegetable metaphor to describe the organicity of the literary work of genius. Young's *Conjectures on Original Composition* (1759) is a plea for textual organicity, recommending originality, individuality, and character rather than rule-bound poetics. Young juxtaposes the rhetoric of Learning with that of genius and its freedom, and considers the formal frameworks defined and regulated by precepts as inhibiting, imposing restraint on the flow of creative energy. He uses architectural metaphors that link learning with formal and constructed wholeness, whereas genius, overflowing with creative energy, produces organic structures that are natural, uncontrolled by the structures of learning, and representative of the processual flow of creativity rather than the finality of formal perfection. Young welcomes generic experimentation and recommends the use of blank verse as the form that is most appropriate for productions of genius. He emphasizes that an "Original may be said to be of a vegetable nature; it rises spontaneously from the vital root of Genius; it grows, it is not made."[34] According to Young, "the human mind's teeming"[35] must not be controlled by regulatory mechanisms. Like Abraham Cowley, he identifies Pindar as an Addisonian great natural genius who "boasted of his No-learning, calling himself the Eagle, for his Flight above" Learning. His compositions were characterized by novelty and impetuosity; he explored "fresh untrodden ground" and "new thought."[36] The energy of genius is further inspired by enthusiasm and the sublime, for "Enthusiastick Passions in Poetry," John Dennis argued, "are truly admirable, when the greater and more violent they are, the more they show the largeness of Soul, and greatness of Capacity of the Writer."[37]

In *Conjectures*, Young advises poets to seek "new models — genres, styles, dictions, prosodic devices that had been used by writers they admired — as an aid to being different, new and serious."[38] Young's stance toward the liberties that genius could take was shared by Pope, who, in the preface to his translation of the *Iliad*, had defended the poem's irregular structure. Pope read Homer's epic as informed by "Invention" and "a great and fruitful" rather than a "judicious and methodical genius."

He drew on a gardening metaphor to describe Homer's natural genius, for "As in the most regular Gardens, Art can only reduce the beauties of Nature to more regularity." Critics, however, "find it easier for themselves to pursue their Observations through an uniform and bounded Walk of Art, than to comprehend the vast and various Extent of Nature."[39] The vastness and variety of the Homeric epic, therefore, contrast strikingly with carefully planned and formally regulated structures.

In *Night Thoughts* and *Conjectures*, Young expressed his preference for blank verse, echoing a number of early eighteenth-century critics who deployed "a mode of speaking or writing, restrained by numbers, and bounded by regularity, [and] consequently more tedious and difficult." Prose and blank verse, by contrast, were considered "loose, easy, and free from trammels."[40] In the satiric *New Art of Poetry*, "Boeticus" even recommended to the epic poet to "Shun Exactness."[41] Exactness was often understood to consist in the "imitative harmony" of rhyme. Blank verse appears to have had associations with the fragmentary, as is indicated in the preface to a fake medieval poem by Elizabeth Halket Wardlaw. She notes that the reader "must immediately perceive" that *Hardyknute: A Fragment* is "aspiring at the Liberty of Blank Verse" and that it "has all the Air of a Fragment":[42] "It seems to be no more than the beginning of, or, as it were, the first Canto of an Heroick Poem. Our Author had at least form'd to himself a more extensive Plan than that which we find executed."[43]

Blank verse enabled poets to avoid repetitive isometrical stanzas for longer poems. Although the couplet—as an ideal form of balance—could be repetitive, it nevertheless was capable of accommodating diverse meanings and serving the purpose of structuring argument. William Bowman Piper observes that the couplet's "persistent closure is *only one* aspect of the normal metrical organization of the closed couplet. This pause, which divides each couplet from the next, is, indeed, only the strongest in a regular hierarchy of metrical pauses."[44] And Margaret Anne Doody states that the couplet "worked for the poets in place of a closed form. Through the attentive use of it, the poets escaped the restrictions of the elaborate and finite stanza. Couplet verse invites and accommodates narrative, and interprets and represents dramatic voices."[45] J. Paul Hunter has pointed to the "symmetrical shape" that the heroic couplet engenders on the printed page,[46] but it is this shape that often contrasts with the fragmented meaning of the poem. Eric Rothstein observes in this regard that it "does not imply completeness or finality with regard to its subject matter. One can argue, in fact, that its polish often contrasts ironically with the openness of the subject matter which it makes accessible to us but which it cannot tame."[47] The gradual shift in poetics from couplet to enjambment, entailing the "jump" from one line to the next, together with the increased use of blank verse, facilitated a greater openness of form and meaning that is characteristic of the mode of the fragmentary. The fragmentary provided relief to monotony and strict formal adherence to prescriptive generic frameworks. Above all, it embodied the paradox between the ambitious desire to reach perfection and man's fallibility. As such, it is a mode that hovers on the borders of completeness, representing longing for finality, yet always suspending this closure and inviting audience interaction. Blank verse, in this respect, is what Young terms "verse unfallen," a type of verse that still has prelapsarian associations of nature and incorruptible innocence. As eighteenth-century poetic practice demonstrates, blank verse became one of the forms most directly associated, and interacting, with the fragmentary to construct organic poems of "vegetable" genius.

THE PLAN OF THE BOOK

The Fragmentary Poetic offers five chapters in which I explore different uses of the mode in the eighteenth century. Chapter 2, on the "Pindaric" mode, provides a contextualization of the ode and the Pindaric "manner," reading early eighteenth-century criticism not so much in terms of prescriptive generic statements about the form of the ode but as an important source for the exploration of the Pindaric paradox at the heart of the fragmentary. Starting with Abraham Cowley's free "traductions" of Pindar, the chapter examines critical works that helped to popularize and vindicate (despite formalist, historical criticism on the structure of the ode by Gilbert West) the ode's associations with the abrupt, irregular, and incomplete. The first part of the chapter dealing with the theorization of the Pindaric "manner" is followed by analyses of productions by poets ranging from such well-known (academic) authors as Thomas Gray, William Collins, and the Warton brothers to the poems of such fascinating, but underresearched, poets as John Bancks and Anne Finch, Countess of Winchilsea. It is the objective of the chapter to introduce a broad spectrum of poems, which were produced by writers of very different backgrounds, but which were nevertheless united in their (at times, very different) uses of the fragmentary.

The third chapter continues my exploration of the Pindaric mode by examining the eighteenth-century long-poem and its transformation of the epic impulse. Offering a brief exploration of the "decline" of the epic in the eighteenth century, the chapter proceeds to examine such long-poems as Thomson's *The Seasons* and Young's *Night Thoughts*. It is argued that, throughout the century, poets were eager to write primary epic, but that, owing to the general problem of translating orality into scripturality, they, on the whole, did not succeed in imitating the primitive genius of Homer and classical epic. Ranging from such authors as Davenant and Cowley to Thomson and Young, the chapter introduces contextualizing material that makes it possible to understand Glover's popular Patriot epic *Leonidas* as a successful poem of a new epic kind that deployed both description and discourse dynamically in an attempt to emulate the orality of primary, original epic. Above all, the chapter reads the long-poem as the product not of a failure to write epic, but as a new form that was informed by generic experimentation and that in original ways realized poets' visions of poetic production, favoring the descriptive over the discursive and action-led narrative.

Chapter 4 introduces a variety of poems that advertised themselves explicitly (either through their titles or prefatory material) as fragments. Like some long-poems, these fragments established a relationship with canonic works to validate their own status. While the first part of the chapter focuses on the contextualizations of pseudo-Spenserian "cantos," the second part explores eighteenth-century authors' attempts at constructing an epic not only by inference but also by national identity. Elizabeth Halket Wardlaw's *Hardyknute*, Thomas Percy's *Five Pieces of Runic Poetry* and *Reliques of Ancient Poetry*, and James Macpherson's *Fragments of Ancient Poetry* are read in terms of their deployment of the fragmentary mode in order to construct a context in which they are understood not only as part of a lost epic but also as a monument of an identity that is being recovered through the publication of these purported fragments. The fifth chapter—with its focus on ruins—considers the importance of the ruinous as a mode that is one of the most popular emanations of the fragmentary. Like the "invented" fragment, the ruin can serve as an emblem of national identity and authority, but it can also become a locus for reflection where the fragmented speaker can collect himself and muse on his existence. The deliberate construction of ruins ought to be comprehended in the same terms as the deliberate writing of fragments and use of the fragmentary. Toward the end of the eighteenth century, the fragmentary becomes a mode centrally preoccupied with matters of identity, as explored in the final chapter on Charlotte Smith's *Beachy Head* and Wordsworth's "Tintern Abbey." In this chapter I relate the Romantic notion of memory to the general sense of disintegration and deracination that pervaded the existence of Smith's hermit figures. Memory serves as a medium through which the broken pieces of the past and past experience, as in Wordsworth's "Pindaric" poem, can be (re)integrated into an imaginative (but no less real and meaningful) whole.

The versions of the fragmentary that are introduced in this study go beyond an exclusive engagement with identity, dealing with questions of authenticity, poetics, the past, and the cultural and literary heritage.[48] The mode of the fragmentary in the eighteenth century constantly puzzles about its own status and invents various mechanisms to legitimize itself. The publication of anthologies, which included compositions reflecting the mode, the establishing of anthologizing methods by Tottel and Dryden, and the popularization of the Longinian sublime (and Dennis's and Burke's interpretations of it) facilitated the dissemination of the fragmentary, and enabled writers to use the mode and apply it to such genres as had traditionally been defined by Aristotelian unity. Inspired in part by poets' inability to imitate the ancients in a way that preserved classical notions of wholeness, the fragmentary permeated all major genres, and aided the process of generic invention and experimentation. *The Fragmentary Poetic* not only aims to offer readings and contextualizations of structures and methods of incompletion, discontinuity, and the resistance to closure so prominent in the poetry of the century, but it also makes a case for the re-reading of much neglected poetry, which will ultimately culminate in a better understanding of both the literary landscape in the period and the boundaries that (in terms of poetics) apparently separate eighteenth-century poets from their Romantic successors.

2
The "Pindaric" Mode

L'ode, avec plus d'éclat et non moins d'énergie
Elévant jusqu'au ciel son vol ambitieux,
Entretient dans ses vers commerce avec les dieux.
Son style impétueux souvent marche au hasard:
Chez elle un beau désordre est un effort de l'art.
— Boileau, *Art Poétique* (1674)

THE ELUSIVE AND FUGITIVE CHARACTER OF CLASSICAL GENRES SUCH AS the ode, which was appropriated first through translations and then adopted as a genre in its own right into English literature, frequently used associations of the fragmentary; in fact, the discourse of the sublime—in texts such as Addison's *The Spectator* and translations of Longinus—helped to legitimize the fragmentary and the unfinished as modes that were representative of, and could inspire, sublimity. In that regard, Sophie Thomas notes that the "fragment is the 'form' of formlessness" and that it "is related to the sublime in so far as it represents what eludes representation, and conveys a limitlessness that cannot be reduced to a concrete finite, or present object."[1] Annamaria Sportelli similarly observes: "Sublime intensity can be described as the visible counterpart of that which cannot be seen, indistinct wholeness, i.e. that expanded space which overcomes the finite nature of the poetic form."[2] It is therefore a mode that is ideally suited to the fragment.

This chapter argues that the major lyric genre of the century—the ode—utilized and popularized the fragmentary and made it accessible to poets who appropriated it to their own generic experiments. Eighteenth-century writers of odes frequently referred to the "manner" and not the "form" of Pindaric odes. The difficulty of rendering Pindar's Epinician odes into English, the lack of knowledge of Greek, and the fragmentary manner of the odes that (through their performative co-

26

herence) would have been understood by the original audience to whom the odes were recited, vaguely encouraged an identification of the ode with the irregular, fragmentary, and the sublime.[3] This definitional confusion facilitated an absorption of the term into a field of "popular" poetics in which any poem, characterized by digression, fragmentariness, and sublimity, could be termed "Pindaric."

THE PINDARIC ODE AS
A FRAGMENTARY GENRE

The emphasis on the "spirit" of the Pindaric ode was first introduced through Abraham Cowley's so-called "traductions." In his "Life of Cowley" (1668), Thomas Spratt describes Cowley's fascination with Pindar as rooted in an interest in the "height of his [Pindar's] Invention."[4] Spratt commends the "boldness of his Metaphors, and the length of his Digressions." The "irregularity of numbers" in the poet's rendering of Pindar, as well as the "frequent alteration of the Rhythm, and Feet," according to Spratt, affect "the mind with a more various delight, while it is soon apt to be tyr'd by the settled pace of any one constant measure." The continual mention of digressions in criticism of the ode (and the long-poem, as will be demonstrated in the next chapter) highlights the importance of digressions as essential characteristics of discontinuous form in that sequential or chronological order is replaced by associative unity that rejects a clearly defined formalist framework. Importantly, however, digressions are not seen as secondary, an afterthought, or additional reflections, but they become integral to the meaning of the composition and contribute to the realization of the design of the fragmentary *Gesamtkunstwerk*.

In the "Preface to Pindarique Odes" (1656), Cowley writes of his rendering of the poetry of Pindar in terms of prose, for "*Critics* have laboured to reduce his [Pindar's] Verses into regular feet and measures . . . yet in effect they are little better than *Prose* to our Ears."[5] Spratt similarly remarks that "this loose, and unconfin'd measure [of prose] has all the Grace, and Harmony of the most confin'd. . . . it is so large and free, that the practice of it will only exalt, not corrupt our Prose."[6] Although this is stated with reference to Cowley's poetic "traductions," it could equally well be regarded as a plea for blank verse.

In his ode on "The Praise of Pindar," Cowley states that "*Pindar* is imitable by none."[7] He describes Pindar's poetic technique in terms of a force that breaks through its natural boundaries, for "*Pindars unnavigable Song* / Like a swoln *Flood* from some steep *Mountain* pours along." Pindar's counteraction of ideals of restraint and control is reworked in the second stanza of Cowley's ode:

> So *Pindar* does new *Words* and *Figures* roul
> Down his impetuous *Dithyrambique Tide*,
>> Which in no *Channel* deigns t'abide,
>> Which neither *Banks* nor *Dikes* controul.
>> Whether th'*Immortal Gods* he sings
> In a no less *Immortal strain*,
> Or the great Acts of *God-descended Kings*,
> Who in his Numbers still survive and *Reign*.
>
> (12–19)

Cowley's coupling of Pindar's novelty with his inability to follow a pre-scribed "Channel" contrasts strikingly with the prescriptivist stance that Thomas Parnell adopted in *An Essay on the Different Stiles in Poetry* (1713). Parnell argued that "Method" was to exert control over "Thought" and that "smooth transition" should connect one part of a poem with another,[8] a stance that was challenged throughout the century with regard to the highest form of the lyric, the Pindaric ode. Similarly, John Dennis, as a partisan of regularity, insisted in *The Grounds of Criticism in Poetry* (1704) that poetry can only fulfill its didactic function if it be regular; for, "if the end of Poetry be to instruct and reform the World, that is, to bring Mankind from Irregularity, Extravagance and Confusion, to Rule and Order, how this should be done by a thing that is itself irregular and extravagant, is difficult to be conceived."[9] By mid-century, however, with a greater interest in Milton and blank verse, this insistence on rhyme had become less predominant and exclusive. In fact, Joseph Addison in *Spectator* no. 477 (1712) could already write of the "Pindaric Manner" in landscape gardening, meaning "the beautiful Wildness of Nature" and implicitly opposing it to the French classicism of symmetrical gardens.[10]

The widely held view among eighteenth-century poets and critics alike was that the greater ode in the style of Pindar was reflective of ir-regularity and fragmentation. Margaret Anne Doody provides a modern evaluation of the sense of fragmentariness and elusiveness of the Pindaric ode that its first critics identified:

> The "Pindaric Ode," so firmly associated with greatness and freedom,
> answered to the Augustan wish for unconstricted versing, formless

form. From the outset, the Pindaric Ode was associated with freedom, lofty manner and intensity of feeling, and with escape from a set or exact verse form. Part of the point of an Augustan Ode is that the reader cannot predict in advance what rhyme pattern may be used; the reading of one stanza or section will not tell us what patterns are to ensue. The stanzas are themselves large and irregular sections or paragraphs of poetry, that may not be matched in rhyme scheme or metre by any other such section, and these sections (which often have little to do with the real Greek divisions of Strophe and Antistrophe) are much longer and apparently require us to take much more in than do quatrains or couplets.[11]

One of the first critics defending the Pindaric ode against the charge of irregularity, lack of method, and its counteraction of neoclassical ideals of harmony and judgment was Charles Gildon. As early as 1718, he complained of the corruption of the Pindaric ode, noting at the same time that "our ignorant Imitators of Pindar have run into a strange inequality and irregularity of Verse, yet it is without Authority from Pindar, whose Odes are perpetually divided by a regular Order."[12] Gildon identified the ideal but at the same time acknowledged poetic practice that favored the fragmentary. The argument provided by Gildon concerning the completeness, perfection, and the "regular Order" of Pindar's compositions is not representative of eighteenth-century theorists of Pindar generally, as, according to Penelope Wilson, few of these commentators "too much trouble to look back to Pindar himself."[13] Gildon (unlike Gilbert West, a critic writing two decades later) does not elaborate on the meter or the exact pattern of division that the Greek poet chose to use, but concentrates on the logical structure in which "Judgment" moderates the "Rapidity of his Fancy." So:

> if we consult Pindar, we shall find that in the midst of [the] Rapidity of his Fancy, Judgment still holds the Reins; and when he rambles, and when he returns from his beautiful Digressions, Judgment every where conducts him.[14]

Gildon's notion of "Judgment" reflects his attempt to introduce an ordering principle into the otherwise irregular and unregulated "manner" of the Pindaric ode. Defining the ode, Gildon observes that the "Pindaric Ode in its Original is distinguish'd from all other Odes by the happy Transitions and Digressions, with which it gains a new Beauty, as well as the surprising, easy, and natural Returns to the Subject, which Graces are not to be attain'd without great Judgment and Genius."[15] Similarly, John Ogilvie, in "An Essay on the Lyric Poetry of the Ancients" (1762), characterized the lyric poet as taking "a more diversified and extensive range," arguing that "his imagination required a strong and steady rein to correct its vehemence, and restrain its rapidity."[16]

Gildon's defense of Pindar is ineffective, since he is unable to reconcile the phenomenon of the poetic liberties that Pindar takes in using "happy Transitions and Digressions" with the ideals of coherence and cohesion, though not necessarily the ideal of closure.[17] He speaks of a "new" kind of "Beauty"—that is, a type of beauty that is created through the counteracting of prescriptive poetics. Like Shakespeare, Spenser, and Milton, Pindar is evaluated in terms of original genius by Gildon. He is, to use Joseph Addison's phrase, a "great natural genius" who did not need formal precepts to produce original works. Modern, as opposed to ancient, genius, far from being able to reject Pindar's poetry as inferior, has to find (or invent) a set of categories that admit of accepting him, even if that entails appraising him not on the basis of contemporary eighteenth-century aesthetics. The element of the "surprising" should be noted, too, since it implies the spontaneity that transcends the plan on which eighteenth-century poetry is usually written.

Edward Young's Preface to *Ocean. An Ode* (1728) synthesizes early eighteenth-century theories of the ode and offers an example of the genre that links it with blank verse. Like Gildon before him, Young highlights the paradoxical nature of the ode:

> The Ode, as it is the Eldest kind of Poetry, so is it the more Spirituous, and more remote from Prose than any other, in Sense, Sound, Expression, and Conduct. It's [*sic*] thoughts should be uncommon, sublime, and moral; Its numbers full, easy, and most harmonious; Its expression pure, strong, delicate, yet unaffected; and of a curious felicity beyond other Poems; Its conduct should be rapturous, somewhat abrupt, and immethodical to a vulgar Eye. That apparent order, and connection, which gives form, and life to some compositions, takes away the soul of this. Fire, elevation, and select thoughts, are indispensable; an humble, tame, and vulgar Ode is the most pitiful error a pen can commit.[18]

The ode has to counteract fixed expectations and to surprise readers through its boldness, for it "is the genuine character, and true merit of the *Ode*, a little to startle some apprehensions."[19] The effect of this boldness, Young admits, can resemble madness. On the one hand, Pindar's style is characterized by being "stately, imperious" and "intoxicating," giving the imagination "the appearance of domineering," whilst on the other, "the *Judgment*, like an Artful Lover, in reality carries its point; and the less it is suspected of it, It shews the more masterly conduct, and deserves the greater commendation."[20] The paradoxical character of the ode—creating an effect of rupture, irregularity, and fragmentation while simultaneously being structured and planned—leads Young to focus on the elements between which eighteenth-century critics of the ode would vacillate in their generic interpretation of it. He, therefore, notes that the

> *Ode* should be *peculiar*, but not *strain'd*; *moral*, but not *flat*; *natural*, but not *obvious*; *delicate*, but not *affected*; *noble*, but not *ambitious*; *full*, but not *obscure*; *fiery*, but not *mad*; *thick*, but not *loaded* in its Numbers, which should be most *Harmonious*, without the least sacrifice of *expression*, or of *sense*. Above all, in *this*, as in every work of Genius, somewhat of an *Original* Spirit should be, at least, attempted.[21]

Young's ambivalence about the principal generic constituents of the ode is echoed in a preface to a one-shilling pamphlet of odes by the obscure poet Richard Barnett, where the author states that he combines blank verse with the genre of the Pindaric ode:

> I call it an Ode; tho' the greatest part of it is Blank Verse: but as I cannot produce any Authorities for this kind of mixture of Blank Verse and Rhyme in the same Piece; I am apprehensive that it will disgust a sort of Critics, who, wanting the sensibility to *feel* the Beauties and Deformities of Poetry, are for reducing every Composition to the exact Standard of Writers whom they approve, merely because it would disgrace the Judgment to own they do not relish them. This kind of Critics would be better pleased to find the Strophe, and Antistrophe, than the Spirit of *Pindar*: for many there are, no Doubt, incapable of feeling a sublime or pathetic Stroke, who can yet count their Fingers with tolerable Accuracy.[22]

The "tolerable Accuracy," however, clearly contrasts with the Pindaric mode, which, according to Richard Shepherd, echoing earlier critics, "requires bold Digressions, [and] abrupt and hasty Transitions."[23]

While most critics of the first half of the century highlight the digressive and formally fragmentary manner of the ode, Henry Pemberton stresses the importance of a diction that is daring. In *Observations on Poetry* (1738), Pemberton, referring to the sublime nature of the Pindaric ode, pointed out that of "all kinds of descriptive poetry the sublime ode requires the boldest diction; strength and a glaring brightness of expression being necessary to support this rapturous kind of verse."[24] The boldness to which he refers reflects the deliberate authorial intention of subverting ideals of formal moderation. Pemberton has in mind a form of poetic discourse that challenges the existing ideals of Horatian order, organization, and the division into stanzas that are regular. Instead, the "rapturous" boldness that he indicates is the expression of the sublime in which the proto-Wordsworthian "overflow of powerful feelings"[25] is not restrained or in any way regularized. Pemberton's aesthetics of boldness is an outspoken preference for the discourse of the sublime in that he rejects Pope's "Nature methodised" and aims at the unmediated expression of enthusiastic emotions and immediacy, which are not directed through the channels of contemplation and aesthetic refinement. Finally, Pemberton notes that it is the sublime and the "human passions with their greatest irregularities"[26] that should be the poet's theme. Other critics, in prefaces to collections, made apologies for the "escapes of a Poetical Genius, which, however suppressed, has at Times shot out into such Luxuriances,"[27] publishing these "Luxuriances" nevertheless and, in doing so, contributing to legitimizing them. By the time Hugh Blair published the *Lectures on Rhetoric and Belles Lettres* (1783), it appears to be an accepted commonplace that the Pindaric is a mode akin to the fragmentary: Blair notes that Pindar "is perpetually digressive and fills up his Poems with Fables of the Gods and Heroes, that have little connection either with his subject, or with one another,"[28] thereby emphasizing the "discontinuous form" that Kenshur comprehends as the defining characteristic of the fragment.

When, later in the century, critics speak of the fugitive and of enthusiasm breaking loose, they have in mind the poetic attempt at finding both a new form of expression and a mode that depart from the aesthetics of imitative harmony of the earlier decades of the century. The rhetoric that some critics use is expressive of the force with which genius reacts to the mechanistic attempt at confining inspiration. The moment when genius manifests itself becomes a poetic event, and the concept of poetic permanence is gradually given up in favor of a view that highlights the spontaneity, abruptness, and violence of poetic creation. In mid-century poetry a shift in emphasis from "sentimental" to "verbal" harmony" occurred. Daniel Webb, in line with Dennis's poetics of rhyme, formulated this distinction between "verbal" and "sentimental" harmony in *Remarks on the Beauties of Poetry* (1762):

The sole aim of versification is harmony. To understand this properly, we must divide it into two kinds. The first consists in a general flow of verse, most pleasing to the ear, but independent of the sense; the second, in bringing the sound or measure of the verse to correspond with, and accompany the idea. The former may be called a verbal harmony; the latter a sentimental.[29]

Incidentally, the blank verse of Thomson's *The Seasons* was frequently criticized for its "verbal harmony."[30] Despite Webb's persistent claim that rhyme was necessary, one of the major writers of odes, William Collins (following Milton) had popularized the "blank ode" with his "Ode to Evening" in 1746 already, demonstrating that harmony could be achieved, even without rhyme. Furthermore, as the titles of numerous collections of poetry demonstrate, "fugitive poetry"[31] — that is, poetry resisting the clearly defined structural regularity that Dennis considers essential in a valuable (meaning didactic) composition — became more popular as the century progressed and the mode of the fragmentary was disseminated through a number of genres. Nick Groom, writing about Thomas Chatterton's fragmentary compositions, explains that the opening or breaking down of generic boundaries of form not only introduces a greater complexity of art production but also threatens the prescriptivist stances of critics like Dennis and Webb.[32] Robert Dodsley, in his anonymously published *The Art of Poetry* of 1741 likewise notes that the ideals of Horatian regularity (especially in the shape of isometrical stanzas) and moderation were not at all unquestioned, pronouncing that "THAT Bard, who follows Horace is undone: / Detest his Practice, and his Precepts shun."[33] Leonard Welsted, in his "Dissertation Concerning the Perfection of the English Language and the State of Poetry," had already argued that the "externals or form" of a poem were less important than its "spirit."[34]

Critics — albeit not universally — recognized both the proselike qualities of Cowley's so-called translations of Pindar's odes and the fragmentary impulse as defining features of the irregular ode in the eighteenth century, so that Gilbert West, in his edition of Pindar's *Olympian Odes* (1749), saw the necessity to comment on the false belief that Pindaric odes were irregular and fragmented:

I must insist that very few . . . not excepting even those written by the admired Mr. Cowley, whose Wit and Fire first brought them into Reputation, have the least Resemblance to the Manner of the Author, whom they pretend to imitate, and from whom they derive their Name.[35]

West opposes the definition of the Pindaric ode that William Congreve had provided in his "Essay on the Pindaric Ode" (1706). Congreve had held that "the character of these late Pindaricks is a Bundle of rambling Thoughts, expressed in a like Parcel of irregular Stanzas, which also consist of such another Complication of disproportioned, uncertain, and perplexed Verses and Rimes."[36] Unlike Cowley and Congreve, West defends the regular structure of Pindaric odes, pointing out that "though his Digressions are frequent, and his Transitions sudden, yet is there ever some secret Connexion, which, though not always appearing to the Eye, never fails to communicate itself to the understanding of the Reader."[37] He then discusses the structural division of the ode into strophe, antistrophe, and epode:

> *You must know that the Ancients (in their Odes) framed two larger Stanzas, and one less; the* first *of the* large Stanzas *they call* Strophe, *singing it on their Festivals at the Altars of the Gods, and dancing at the same Time. The* second *they call* Antistrophe, *in which they inverted the Dance. The* lesser Stanza *was named the* Epode, *which they sung standing still. The* Strophe, *as they say, denoted the Motion of the* higher Sphere, *the* Antistrophe *that of the* Planets, *the* Epode *the fixed station and Repose of the* Earth. . . . *The first and second Stanzas [strophe and antistrophe] contained always the same Number and the same kind of verses. The* Epode *was of a different Length and Measure; and if the Ode run out into any Length, it was always divided into* Triplets of Stanzas, *the two first being constantly of the same Length and Measure, and all the* Epodes *in the like manner corresponding exactly with each other, from all which the Regularity of this kind of Compositions is sufficiently evident.*[38]

West observes that the effect of structural incompleteness can be counteracted by means of the transitions and connections that are established through the performative aspect of the ode, which he characterizes as "a Poem intended to be sung in Publick."[39] This public, as well as communal, aspect echoes the communal making and recitation of primary epic and the traditional ballad; at the same, it also uses the fragmentary implications of abrupt transitions that a spontaneous making of the text entails. In the majority of ode writers' productions, however, West's theory of the ode was opposed by an attempt to capture the manner of Pindar.

Poets such as William Collins and Mark Akenside repeatedly used the tripartite division to which West refers in his Preface; Collins even structures his odes in accordance with the classical hymnal scheme of *invocatio, pars epica* and final petition that Kurt Schlüter regards as the closest approximation of the prayer hymn, the *hymnos kleticos*. Collins primarily uses a thematic division and not the structural or metrical division that West suggests. In spite of West's emphasis on Pindaric regularity, mid-eighteenth-century poetics hailed the supposedly formal freedom embodied by Greek literary culture as far preferable to its Latin equivalent.[40] Mid-century poets then added to this ideational freedom the individualized treatment of form by opening and relaxing their understanding of unity, coherence, and proportion. This, of course, led to a weakening of definitional boundaries as well as a frequent recurrence to modal rather than structural features to denominate a genre.

Ralph Cohen suggests that the ode as a generic construct not only comprised the Pindaric or sublime ode on matters of public importance, but also the lesser ode. The latter was derived from, modeled on, and inspired by Horace's odes and epodes and used the classically Roman ideals of regularity and polish. Cohen demonstrates that mid-century users of the lesser ode included ballads, songs, and shorter compositions like elegies, as well as sonnets among those poems they termed "odes": "Odes could be composed of numerous particular species; ode, therefore, whether 'sublime' or 'lesser', was a collective designation, a genus which contained numerous species."[41] The ode was a variable genre and could include long religious poems such as Young's *Ocean* or descriptive productions like John Dyer's "Grongar Hill." Numberless tonal variations occur within the genre, variations that are reflected by the various subspecies of the ode such as epithalamia, Anacreontics, Sapphics, and others.

Robert Mayo, writing of the final decades of the eighteenth century, describes the changes affecting genre and modes in the period that can equally be identified in the literature of the earlier decades of the century. According to Mayo, the later eighteenth century "was a period of great confusion with respect to traditional literary genres—a period which was witnessing widespread dislocations in literary taste, and a corresponding shift in opinion concerning the true nature of poetry."[42] The ode was a generic term that admitted of a definitional freedom that other forms like the sonnet could not offer. Nathanial Teich, in that regard, remarks that "in many cases, generic conventions provided increasingly fewer rigid operational choices for poets and less predictable products for readers and critics."[43] While Cohen's observation regarding the versatility and the poet's understanding of the generically open conceptualization of the ode is valid, it does not take into account that the fragmentary mode interacts with modes such as the sublime. Odes use the sudden transitions and digressions ascribed to Pindar to evoke ideas of the fragmentary and the sublime. This modal characteristic of the ode leads critics such as Paul H. Fry to insist on a thematic definition of the ode, arguing that the ode is a "celebratory poem of address in elevated language written on occasions of public importance."[44] West's definition of the ode—although the most sophisticated in the eighteenth century—had little impact on the understanding and use of the Pindaric "manner," a manner that commonly relies on the hymnal elements of the ode.[45] The great advantage of the Pindaric mode over structurally defined forms such as the sonnet was that it was inclusive and accommodating, as Cohen has pointed out, rather than exclusive and limiting.

READING THE FRAGMENTARY IMPULSE

What follows is an exploration of a number of poems, which can be loosely classified as odes and which illustrate in numerous ways the "Pindaric" or fragmentary mode discussed so far. As a matter of fact, the majority of odes in the eighteenth century do not follow the strict hymnal scheme of the traditional prayer hymn but attempt nevertheless the sublimity so characteristic of the greater ode.

William Hamilton of Bangour (1704–54), a Scottish Jacobite, poet, and propagandist, included two lyric fragments in his *Poems on Several Occasions* (1748), "The Flowers. A Fragment" and "Doves. A Fragment."[46] Hamilton "combined the inheritance of a classical education with a sensitivity to his country's culture," and took part in the "vernacular revival"[47] by producing ballads hailing a glorious Scottish past that stood in clear contrast to the enforced Union between the two kingdoms. His use of the fragmentary in *Poems*, however, is inspired by the fragment productions that were published in Anglo-Scottish miscellanies such as Allan Ramsay's *The Evergreen*. "Doves. A Fragment" makes use of the associative technique so typical of the ode. The fragment is divided into three parts, and is open-ended since the reader is not informed of the invoked lover's response to the speaker's address:

> Of DOVES sweet gentle birds, the heaven born Muse
> Prepares to sing, their manners and what law,
> The blameless race obey, their cares and loves.
> O sacred VIRGIN, that, to me unseen
> Yet present, whispers nightly in my ear
> Love dited song or tale of martial Knight,

As best becomes the time: and aidful grants
Celestial grace implor'd, O, bounteous, say
What fav'rite maid in her first bloom of youth
Wilt chuse to honour? Seem I not to see
The laurel shake, and hear the voice divine
Sound in mine ear: 'With Erskine best agrees
'The song of Doves: herself a dove, well pleas'd
'Listen gracious to the tale benign, and hear
'How the chaste bird with word's [*sic*] of fondling love,
'Soft billing, woo's his maid, their spousal loves,
'Pure and unstain'd with jealous fear of change;
'How studious they to build their little nests
'Nature's artificers! And tender, breed
'Their unfledg'd children, till they wing their flight,
'Each parent's care.' Come, as the Muse ordains,
O thou of every grace, whose looks of love,
Erskine, attractive, draw all wond'ring eyes
Constant to gaze; and whose subduing speech
Drops as the honey comb, and grace is pour'd
Into thy lips: for ever thee attends
Sweetness thy handmaid, and, with beauty, clothes
As with the morning's robe invested round:
O come, again invok'd, and smiling lend
Thy pleas'd attention, whilst in figure'd silk
Thy knowing needle plants th' embroider'd flower
As in its native bed: so may'st thou find
Delight perpetual and th' inclining ear
Of heav'n propitious to thy maiden vow,
When thou shalt seek from Love a youth adorn'd
With all perfection, worthy of thy choice,
To bless thy night of joy and social care.
O happy he, for whom the vow is made.

. . . .

The initial part of the fragment is narrative and introduces the general information that the Muse is about to produce a song about doves and their symbolic meaning in the context of love. The Muse's "Celestial grace" reproduces "Love dited song or tale of martial Knight," and in lines 12–21 the speaker, through direct speech, introduces the Muse's song, which deals with the "fondling love" of two doves, their mating, and joint effort to construct a symbol of their union and love — that is, a nest in which their "unfledg'd children" are to be reared. Rather abruptly, line 21 ends this interspersed song and re-introduces the speaker's voice. The more general introductory part concerning the Muse and the succeeding song are here followed by a personal address of the speaker's lover. While the depiction of "fondling love" was dealt with metaphorically in the Muse's song, the speaker invokes his beloved in terms that are expressive of his desire to emulate the doves' love. He has provided the Muse's song and has applied it to his own longing for a girl that is characterized by sweetness, mildness, and constancy. The open-ended character of the fragment and the speaker's attempt at convincing the girl to accept him as a lover are expressed by the asterisks at the end of the composition. Certainly, the last part of this poetic fragment appears disjunctive and unbalanced. It counteracts the structural proportion that had been established with parts 1 and 2. Yet, it is this disproportionate character of the potentially endless third part that is used again and again in poetic fragments of the eighteenth century.

Better known than his countryman, William Hamilton, David Mallet (1705–65), Anglo-Scottish patriot poet, playwright, and a close friend of James Thomson, was a prolific author, and his works were frequently anthologized. He was attracted to the Pindaric impulse and produced works in those genres that were clearly associated with modal fragmentariness—the ode and the long-poem—using the fragmentary in his long-poems, *The Excursion* and *Amyntor and Theodora* and his dream-vision "Truth in Rhyme." His "A Fragment" was printed in the Oxford anthology, *The Union: or, Select Scots and English Poems* (1753), which was edited by Thomas Warton, later Oxford Professor of Poetry and author of *Observations on the Fairy Queen*.[48] Warton's collection, according to David Nichol Smith, was one of the most successful minor miscellanies of the century, but, more important, it "represent[ed] the taste of a young scholar who took a discriminating pleasure in the poetry of his contemporaries, and himself exemplified the new trend."[49] It contained a number of poems relevant for this study: a variety of odes by the most important poets of the day, ballads, and (among other poems excerpted from Allan Ramsay's *The Evergreen*) Lady Wardlaw's *Hardyknute*, poems that draw on the strategies of the fragmentary to authenticate themselves in terms of their antiquity. Mallet's poem, which had first been published in his collection of poems of 1743, follows the traditional hymnal structure of classical odes. The first stanzaic unit, however, differs from the remaining units in that it does not adhere to the classical structure otherwise used throughout the poem. It is preoccupied with the sublime and deals with ideas such as infinity and diffusion. Thus, again, in this mid-century production, the ideational aspects of the fragment and sublimity are foregrounded in favor of a deliberate attempt at counteracting poetic closure. The text of the first stanza is here reproduced in full:

> FAIR morn ascends: soft zephyr's wing
> O'er hill and vale renews the spring:
> Where, sown profusely, herb and flower,
> Of balmy smell, of healing power,
> Their souls in fragrant dews exhale,
> And breathe fresh life in every gale.
> Here, spreads a green expanse of plains,
> Where, sweetly-pensive, Silence reigns;
> And there, at utmost stretch of eye,
> A mountain fades into the sky;
> While winding round, diffus'd and deep,
> A river rowls with sounding sweep.
> Of human art no traces near,
> I seem alone with Nature here!
>
> (1–14)

The poem opens as a reflection on the symbolism of a new morning and then turns into a description of the physical appearance of the landscape. The "green expanse of plains" is rather vague, but stresses that the speaker's perception can hardly capture and comprehend the vastness of the landscape, an idea that is echoed in the poet's mention of the limit that his sight has reached in looking at the mountain. The "utmost stretch of eye" is expressive not only of the poet's intention of exploring spaces but also of discovering contact zones and border lines. He is interested in those parts of the perceived landscape that he cannot clearly see. As the "mountain fades into the sky," the speaker follows it imaginatively. His imagination has to produce a continuation of the visual representation of the mountain since the mountain "fades" into the sky and is therefore not properly visible to the speaker. Furthermore, he has to apprehend what he is not able to perceive visually. The fading of clearly perceptible objects, in that sense, stands for the loss of definite outlines, as well as of an organized structure. The wide "expanse of plains," similarly, also indicates that the well-organized structure of human thinking is counteracted by a natural fragmentation of the landscape. Nature's effect on man is overwhelming, and man has to try to follow striking features in the landscape in order to establish a compositional scheme in his mind. The river winds "diffus'd and deep," and it also fragments a landscape that, like mid-eighteenth-century landscape gardens, possessed "natural" rivulets, vistas, and shrubs that *appeared* natural but had nevertheless been planned artfully. Mallet notes at the end of the stanza that there appears to be no trace of "human art." The poem's meaning is translated into its form, morphing through the mode of the fragmentary into discrete features that, in the reading process, need to be spontaneously and imaginatively connected by the speaker. While Mallet's fragment was no doubt influenced by his engagement with the sublime, he did not historicize the contents of his poem to vindicate the fragmentary. This type of vindication, however, is often found with "university" and antiquarian poets.

Among academic poets favoring the fragmentary, Thomas Gray (1716–71), Professor of Modern History at Cambridge University, deserves special mention. Warton included Gray's celebrated "Elegy Written in a Country Churchyard" in *The Union* and thereby placed it in the company of pseudo-ancient productions such as *Hardyknute*. Throughout his life, Gray was interested in literary history and carried out extensive research into Welsh and Old Norse poetry. In 1768 he published, alongside two odes, "The Fatal Sisters" and "The Descent of Odin," an imitative fragment entitled "The Triumph of Owen. A Fragment." The accompanying advertisement situates the fragment within the context of such antiquarian publications as Evan Evans's *Specimens of the Poetry of the Ancient Welch Bards* (1764). James Mulholland states that "Gray develops and refines a poetics of 'printed voice,'" attempting to capture orality through print, and that he "approximates in his poetry some of the formal characteristics of oral culture in order to foster a sense of immediacy between himself and his readers."[50] The printed rendering of a comprehensive experience of an event such as the bard's suicide in *The Bard* (1757) relies on its open-endedness for dramatic effect; the fragmentary highlights a climactic point by presenting only a glimpse of the action and minimal contextual material. Mulholland notes that "Gray refers to this poem ["The Triumph of Owen"] as a fragment, accentuating his imagined role as an editor who has selected part of a text rather than as author who has created it,"[51] but does not recognize Gray's specific use of the mode of the fragmentary.

"The Triumph of Owen" forms part of a series of fragment poems that Gray produced in imitation of Old Norse poetry. It is reminiscent of the poetic prose of Macpherson's Ossian compositions in that "OWEN's praise demands" the bard's "song." The bardic singer whose honor and station Gray had celebrated in his Pindaric ode, *The Bard*, sets out to praise the heroism of "OWEN swift, and OWEN strong":

> Fairest flower of Roderic's stem,
> Gwyneth's shield, and Britain's gem.
> He nor heaps his brooded stores,
> Nor on all profusely pours;
> Lord of every regal art,
> Liberal hand, and open heart.
>
> (3–8)

Interestingly, the singer's identity as a druidic bard is revealed in line 1, before the subject is introduced. There appears to be an imbalance between the praise that the bard is to articulate and the semantic and syntactical stress on "my song." What follows are three heterometrical stanzas. While the speaker's voice was prominent in the first line, it does not appear again in the rest of the poem; the possessive pronoun "my" of the beginning denoted individual subjectivity. By contrast, the abruptness and shortness of words at the end of the fragment are expressive of the bard's position within the poem: apart from being a mere observer who records the deeds of the valiant Owen, he has to accompany the hero, witness his actions, and expose himself to the same dangers that Owen has to face.

According to Gray:

> Where he [Owen] points his purple spear,
> Hasty, hasty Rout is there,
> Marking with indignant eye
> Fear to stop, and shame to fly.
> There Confusion, Terror's child,
> Conflict fierce, and Ruin wild,
> Agony, that pants for breath,
> Despair and honourable Death.
> . . . .
>
> (29–36)

The poem ends with three asterisks, indicating, perhaps, that Owen has fulfilled his heroic action or that he (or, what is more important for our understanding of Gray's choice of the fragment form, the bard) has met an "honourable Death" on the battlefield. The bard, like the personification of Agony, seems to "pant for breath," describing the action in largely monosyllabic words. His excitement and fear, as well as his apprehension of the "Ruin wild," manifest themselves in the staccato and abrupt structure of the fragment. The end of the bard's existence has provided the finality that the poem itself lacks—the poem thereby shifts from the depiction of the heroism of Owen to the praise and glorification of the bard's existence and his self-sacrifice as druidic historiographer and sage. In this interpretation, rather than understanding "The Triumph of Owen. A Fragment" as a eulogy on medieval heroism, it is another poem that, like *The Bard*, pays tribute to the druidic singers as essential pillars of Celtic society. Gray makes use of strategies of fragmentation and, notwithstanding his generic choice of the ode, exploits the pseudohistorical representation of "Owen's praise" and relates it to the premature death of the bard in battle, thereby at the same time ending the poem and encouraging the reader to conclude it with a suitable ending in praise of the heroic bard who, while speaking in the ode, dies in battle.

Gray's experiments with the fragmentary are owing to his sensitivity to new trends in both antiquarian scholarship and his use of the Pindaric ode. As an antiquarian, he was interested in ruins and the discourse of fragmentation that was introduced to the disciplines of the humanities; this new interest in the ruinous cross-fertilized these disciplines' preoccupation with the fragmentary. In this light, it seems less surprising that William Mason, Gray's friend, writer of odes, and literary executor, opted for the inclusion of fragmentary poetry in the edition that followed the latter's death. Marjorie Levinson, writing of Mason's posthumous edition of the works of his friend, is intrigued by the editor's defense of his inclusion of fragments in the edition. According to Levinson:

> [the] most interesting aspect of Mason's edition is his determination to defend the propriety of fragment presentation even in a Memoir. Mason's anxiety on this score extends to his treatment of all material not intended for publication. . . . Mason . . . clearly anticipates criticism for his boldness in exposing his author's unfinished work; he averts this censure by protesting the extraordinary perfection to which Gray brought all his poetry. By polishing each unit of writing as he composed it and before proceeding to the next unit, Gray bequeathed to posterity a collection of highly finished fragments in no way capable of embarrassing the poet's finest achievements.[52]

Gray was known for the notorious habit of revising his poetry. The paradoxical nature of Gray's fragments, which are considered as "highly finished fragments," to use Levinson's words, is identifiable in a variety of deliberately conceptualized fragments. This means that, although fragments might have been left unfinished, they may still be associated with, and read against, finished compositions of the author's poetic canon, thereby introducing extratextual criteria of perfection that, as in the case of eighteenth-century artificial ruins, are recontextualized within a paradoxical framework of sublime pseudo-perfection.

THE ODE WRITER'S QUEST FOR
INSPIRATION AND COMPLETENESS

Shaun Irlam understands the ode as an ideal genre for the "moral rejuvenation of literature and modern society and the redemption of mankind from the consequences of the Fall."[53] The ode (especially the hymnal ode of Collins) represents the poet's effort to remedy the fragmentariness of human existence. Through the invocation of the poem's deity, the speaker aims to gain a sense of the greatness, creative force, and spirituality of the goddess who can inspire him. The invocation, in that regard, represents the poetic process of approximating the divine and partaking of the experience of being inspired. The infinite and obscure—represented by the divine—awe the speaker, but they also induce him to attempt to overcome his own limitations as a mortal and petition for a higher existence of one endowed with the powers of grace and the sublime. In that sense, the ode becomes a map of his unfulfilled desires, as well as a reflection of the fragmented state of human existence, a state that precedes the one of inspired immortality. Collins (1721–59) attended the University of Oxford with his Winchester College friend, Joseph Warton, himself the author of a collection of odes, and (probably through the influence of Robert Lowth, the author of *De Sacra Poesi Hebræorum* [1753]) became familiar with theories of the ode that related it to the sublime and sacred. His mythopoeic odes represent an attempt to capture the spirituality of divinities such as Fancy and Eve and a desire to negotiate the imaginative encounter between the human and the heavenly.

Collins's "Ode on the Poetical Character," published in *Odes on Several Descriptive and Allegoric Subjects* (1746), establishes a relationship between the speaker and a goddess (Fancy) who is petitioned and expected to grant the wish for inspiration and admission to "Waller's myrtle shades" that Collins articulates in the epode of his ode. Coleridge confessed that the ode "whirled *me* along with greater agitations of enthusiasm than any the most *impassioned* scene in Schiller or Shakespeare."[54] William Hymers (c.1758–83?), who was preparing an edition of Collins's poetry at the time of his death, noted in his "Preface to the Ode on the Poetical Character" that the "complexion" of the poem is "sacred" and that Collins "does not represent Fancy such as she is feigned to be by the generality of Poets; but makes her that <divine> heavenly Being whom the Almighty himself is delighted to converse with, and who bore a principal part in the formation of the universe."[55] Collins's speaker hopes for a "magic girdle" of inspiration and purity, the "cest of amplest power" with which—through the conjuring powers of Fancy—he can "gaze her visions wild, and feel unmixed her flame." At the end of the poem, he has a vision of the country to which he wants to find access. It is the country of the blind Milton and Spenser:

> Of rude access, of prospect wild,
> Where tangled round the jealous steep,
> Strange shades o'erbrow the valleys deep,
> And holy genii guard the rock,
> Its glooms embrown, its springs unlock,
> While on its rich ambitious head,
> An Eden, like his own, lies spread.[56]
>
> (56–62)

It is an Edenic vision that seems to be impossible for the poet-speaker to access, unless he be granted Fancy's "cest of amplest power." The "cest" endows its bearer with grace, a quality that is related, but superior, to the sublime.[57] Collins is anxious about the possibility of entering the "fancied glades," but, as is evidenced in the "Ode to Evening," is soothed by his communion with the Evening goddess. John Sitter notes with regard to Collins's Eden:

> With the poem's actual survey in mind, the final phrase leaves an odd note in the air; it suggests that perhaps the appropriate emphasis is "from every *future* view," that the ode now being completed, rather than *Paradise Lost*, is the last poetic glimpse of these lands. Whether or not this is so, whether Milton or Milton-in-Collins was really the last man out of Paradise, the full implications of ambition and optimism remain through the end of the poem. In either case, the Edenic stage of English poetry is *now* over, and there is no reason to assume that this fall need be any less fortunate than the biblical fall.[58]

Joseph Warton, the future author of the *Essay on the Genius and Writing of Mr Pope*, in his "Ode to Fancy" (published in the same year as Collins's, in *Odes on Various Subjects*) similarly characterizes Fancy as empowered by an "all-commanding wand, / Of pow'r to bid fresh gardens bloom" and recreate past summer, thereby enabling the poet-speaker to experience "visionary bliss."[59]

While the "Ode on the Poetical Character" represents the speaker's longing for Paradise and the associated bestowal of the cestus as unlikely, the rapport that the speaker develops with Eve in the "Ode to Evening" (an important "blank ode" that was included in Dodsley's *Collection of Poems by Several Hands*) is one of intimacy and hopefulness. Collins's evening ode, rather than merely voicing the hymnal prayer and petition to "breathe some softened strain," can be understood as a love-song for Eve in which the speaker wants to "own" Eve's "gentlest influence"—that is, the influence of love. The extended use of prolepsis in the meandering and ritual invocation to Eve (lines 1–20), as well as the conditional-clause construction at the beginning of the poem, indicate that Collins understood the encounter between the divine and the human as (primarily) possible through the powers of the imagination. His concluding petition, therefore is modest:

> Of these [genius and "divine excess"] let others ask
> > To aid some mighty task:
> I only seek to find thy temperate vale,
> > Where oft my reed might sound
> > To maids and shepherds round,
> And all thy sons, O Nature, learn my tale.
>
> > > > (49–53)

Thomas Warton, Joseph's brother, extends the descriptive-allegoric mode of Collins in the "Ode on the Approach of Summer" (1753). The poem follows the progress of summer but at the end of the ode invokes Summer to allow his speaker to "live true votary" "to sweet Poesy":

> She shall lead me by the hand,
> Queen of sweet smiles, and solace bland!
> She from her precious stores shall shed
> Ambrosial flow'rets o'er my head:
> She from my tender youthful cheek,
> Can wipe, with lenient finger meek,
> The secret and unpitied tear,

> Which still I drop in darkness drear.
> She shall be my blooming bride;
> With her, as years successive glide,
> I'll hold divinest dalliance,
> For ever held in holy trance.[60]
>
> (327–38)

The ode opens with an apostrophe of "iron-scepter'd WINTER" who is asked to withdraw to "bleak Siberian waste" and "polar solitude" in order for the speaker to be able to hail "sweetest SUMMER." Warton provides a pseudo-genealogical history of Summer, denominating April as the surrogate father of Summer, and that he "fed" her "with rare nectarine fruits" so that she eventually "bloom'd a goddess debonair." The speaker introduces the image of Summer being nurtured by April because he—analogically—also desires to be nurtured and transformed from a mere worshipper of summer into an inspired poet, the "votary" of Poesy. Summer (as a metonymical representation of Nature) inspires the speaker with the natural beauty and sublimity of the landscape; he also witnesses Summer's aratological train of sister and tributary deities such as Eve, Health, and "Contemplation hoar" and with Summer's assistance is transported to "yon antique wood, / Dim temple of sage Solitude." At the temple of Solitude, the poet-speaker can pray for the fulfillment of his wish for inspiration, a wish that Warton's speaker also expresses in his ode, "Solitude at an Inn," when he addresses the deity by revealing that "loneliness to me [is] / Best and true society."[61] At the shrine of Solitude, the speaker can indulge in his "musing mood" and perform "many a whisper'd rite" in order for the goddess to grant his petition for inspiration.

The ode abruptly returns to Summer and her ability to inspire rhapsody in the speaker:

> 'Tis thou, alone, O SUMMER mild,
> Can'st bid me carol wood-notes wild:
> Whene'er I view thy genial scenes;
> Thy waving woods, embroider'd greens;
> What fires within my bosom wake,
> How glows my mind the reed to take!
>
> (273–78)

The new day, hailed by the arrival of "mild morn"—as in Thomson's "Hymn to the Seasons"—enables the speaker to experience the divine essence of Nature:

> . . . when mild Morn in saffron stole
> First issues from her eastern goal,
> Let not my due feet fail to climb
> Some breezy summit's brow sublime,
> Whence Nature's universal face
> Illumin'd smiles with new-born grace;
> (255–60)

The speaker translates the morning's "new-born grace" into his song and chants a song of praise for Nature and Summer. The concluding move to the goddess of poetry, Poesy (who had not been mentioned earlier in the poem), is an attempt on the speaker's part to re-enact the rhapsody that Summer (and the summer morning) had enabled him to experience. What he desires most is permanency and a continual experience of the "holy trance," and it is to effect this ability to pray poetically—in the form of the hymnal prayer—that he desires to partake of Poesy's "precious stores." These stores will furnish him with the experience of Summer, even when "gloomy" Winter has usurped the scene. It is the force of the sublime that he experienced through his real encounter with "mild Morn" that he wants to re-experience by means of the imaginative powers of Summer. This force is expressive of a perpetual summer, a prelapsarian state of happiness that knows no change and that Thomson—at the end of *Winter: A Poem*—focused on, in terms of an afterlife and an eternal summer without the strife and suffering of Winter.

The descriptive-allegoric ode frequently used the fragmentary in the sense that an imaginary and sublime Eden could be evoked through a fancied encounter with a divine power. Poets such as William Mason, Gilbert West, Mark Akenside, and James Thomson all wrote odes addressing divinities, and the mode in its mythopoeic emanation was popular up until the 1770s. James Scott (1733–1814), Fellow of Trinity College, Cambridge, clergyman, and author of *Odes on Several Subjects* (1761), in his ode "To the Muse" clearly follows in the footsteps of Collins and the Wartons. As with his predecessors in the hymnal ode, he does not restrict himself to the encomiastic aspect of the ode, but implores the muse to be admitted among her train. Stanza 1 is representative of this desire:

> Yet once more, sweetest Queen of Song,
>   Thy humblest suppliant lead along,
>   Through Fancy's flow'ry plains:
> Or bear me to th'ideal grove,

Where hand in hand the Graces rove,
And sooth me with seraphic strains!
'Tis thine, harmonious Maid, to cull
Delicious balm to heal our cares;
'Tis thine to take the prison'd soul,
And lap it in Elysian airs;
While quick as thought at thy divine command
The realms of grace, and Harmony expand.[62]

(1–12)

Scott's speaker can only overcome the limitations of his human existence if he is admitted by the muse "to th'ideal grove," a supertemporal location where he can experience the "realms of grace" as well as its "Harmony," where the disharmony of mundane human life can be excluded, and where his "cares" can "heal."[63] The supplication demonstrates his inferior position, a position from which he desires to be raised and delivered by the muse. In this "realm" he will be "ravisht" and witness "visionary scenes." He will transcend his own mortality and fragmentariness and become—through his intercourse with the divine—a "momentary god."[64]

Scott was one of the last writers who used the allegorical ode as effectively as the poets of the 1740s did. This type of descriptive-allegoric ode frequently adopted the features of sublimity, pseudo-sacred themes, and Pindaric wildness. While the appearance of abruptness and formal fragmentariness (through complex and, at times, overburdened syntax and prolepsis) is constructed deliberately by poets such as Collins, Akenside, and the Wartons, these features are also expressive of a wider concern: these odes aim to articulate an awareness of the loss of innocence and the consequent necessity to be inspired and to regain originary, Edenic bliss. The speaking self of these mythopoeic odes is aware of the original fall and the consequent loss of perfection (and immortality) that the expulsion from paradise necessitated and hopes to achieve (again) wholeness and completion through the reciprocation or answering of the hymnal invocation.

Mark Akenside (1721–70), a Newcastle physician and author of *The Pleasures of Imagination* (1744), produced a variation on Collins's quest for spiritual completedness by dealing with the theme of cultural degeneration. In his *Odes on Several Subjects* (1745), "Ode XV"—also published as "On Domestic Manners: A Fragment"—follows his reflections on "Meek honour, female shame."[65] In the poem, the speaker deplores the flight of the goddess from Albion and is aware that the disappearance of

"Meek honour" will result in the degeneration of those values of conjugal happiness and health that Akenside praised in his collection:

> our youths in vain
> Concerning nuptial happiness inquire;
> Our maids no more aspire
> The arts of bashful Hymen to attain:
> But with triumphant eyes
> And cheeks impassive, as they move along,
> Ask homage of the throng.
> The lover swears that in a harlot's arms
> Are found the selfsame charms,
> And worthless and deserted lives and dies.
>   (11–20)

The poem's form is regular; it consists of four stanzas with ten lines each. The fragmentary mode of the composition is thematically established through Akenside's elaboration on the effect of cultural degeneration that the goddess' flight from the country has triggered. The last stanza introduces "Britannia's guardian Genius" who encounters the "strife and grief," as well as man's indifference toward the pleasure and security of a well-instructed and morally good family life. The consequence of her indignation at this state of degeneration is that she reveals her "wrath" "with her adamantine spear." The last line, reproduced in brackets, voices the poet's own statement, "I watch'd her awful words and made them mine," but he does not reproduce her words nor does he attempt to become her spokesman, who reveals the true destruction the "guardian Genius" could bring to those who have departed from the standards of "Meek honour." Although he declares himself to be the deity's spokesman (using the personal pronoun "I"), he nevertheless fragments the warning of the goddess by finishing his invocation with a number of elusive asterisks.

THE TWO-PART FRAGMENT

Another kind of "Pindaric" poem (which does not aspire to be an ode), using explicitly the mode and "form" of the unfinished, may be termed the "two-part fragment." It was used by a number of authors who experimented with the fragmentary mode. It consisted of a textual structure that was divided into two parts, the first of which provided a story (a reverie, thought, or reflection) that usually started *in medias res*, with a second part focusing on a reaction or conclusion to what had been presented in the previous part. E. Dower's "The New River Head, a Fragment" (1738) may serve as an example:

> Tired with books and rolling on the bed,
> I walked one evening to the River Head.
> There patient anglers do the fishes tease,
> And dogs are washed to clean them from the fleas;
> From thence you hear the noise of jangling bells,
> Or the soft Italian tunes from Sadler's Wells.
> There citizens tell each other who is the winner,
> And clergy boast of what they had for dinner;
> The lovesick maid from death will not refrain—
> Plunges in there, and laughs at future pain.
> Some walk there to get appetites to their meat,
> And others like me, that has no food to eat.
> From the verdant fields comes a fragrant smell,
> Whilst the gay town looks like the mouth of hell.
>
> —I thought of woods, palaces and springs,
> Riches, poverty and the pomp of kings.
> Whilst th' royal swans for food did seem to weep,
> I leaned upon my staff and fell asleep.[66]

Metrically, Dower, the author of *The Salopian Esquire* (1739), uses the regularity of the couplet dominantly. The first part of the poetic fragment introduces the occasion of the speaker's walk to the River Head— that is, his inability to sleep. What he sees there is then put into a panorama of various unconnected images that are all linked by the speaker's deliberately associating them with the evening. His reflections, however, are not the unique experience of "one evening['s]" visit to the River Head; rather, his thoughts are expressed in general terms and reveal a long acquaintance with the area, as well as with what happens there at night. This tension between the more general tone of the fragment and the particular occasion of his sleeplessness is also expressed grammatically by the poet's use of the simple past tense in the first two lines and his shift toward the simple present for his more general thoughts about the things and people he might have seen there on previous visits.

The final quatrain of the poem is visually separated from the text by a dash. The dash indicates a break and re-introduces the past tense of the second line. It abruptly finishes the description of the various impressions that were combined in his mind and thereby fragments a reverie of numerous associations that might have continued on several pages. In that regard, the last line stating that he has fallen asleep makes clear that the depiction of his thoughts has been completed by his being overcome by sleep. Sleep thus provides the closure that the speaker's presence at the River Head had counteracted—his being exposed to the sight of the River Head inspired reflections that resisted closure and developed digressive autodynamics connecting past experience with the particular occasion of the speaker's looking for rest.

Dower uses the fragment as a special mode of (poetic) narrative in which the introductory lines articulate the occasion and motivation of the speaker's taking a walk to the River Head. The shifting use of tenses further reveals that the speaker is remembering what he did and thought on that particular evening—the framework of the unique experience of the night is constructed in the past tense, whilst the more general associations that the River Head inspires are expressed in a more immediate present tense. The fragmentary character of the poem is highlighted by the immediacy the speaker creates in the middle part of the poem, where he reproduces a whole catalogue of reflections that come to his mind. The (spontaneous) reflections that are triggered by the familiar environment of the River Head resist closure and finality because the speaker is awake, and new images and thoughts are constantly arising in his mind. Only with the temporal finality of sleep will the framework of the poem be complete and the tensions of fragmentation effective.

A production that uses a very similar strategy of fragmentation is John Bancks's (1709–51) "A Fragment."[67] Bancks, according to William J. Christmas, "represents a curious case of plebeian inauthenticity coupled with an aggressive manipulation of popular literary trends, all in the service of writerly ambition and self-promotion."[68] Trying to benefit from the success of Stephen Duck, who, as a laboring-class poet, had received royal patronage, Bancks (who had spent a short period as a weaver's apprentice but then set up a bookstall in Spitalfields) published *The Weaver's Miscellany* in 1730. The subscription-supported *Miscellaneous Works: in verse and prose, of John Bancks* (1738) was more ambitious and demonstrated its author's familiarity with genre theory. Bancks's "A Fragment," like Dower's "The New River Head," also employs a narrative—this time, one that focuses on the speaker's attempt to persuade Cloe to give herself up to him sexually. Apart from an introductory section that uses the past tense to prepare the setting and the general situation of "Cloe's chamber, [where] she and I / Together sat, no creature nigh," the speaker expresses his desire for "the joys of love." This introduction is followed by a dialogue between the speaker and Cloe in which he tries to convince her of his honorable intentions of being hers "forever." The dramatic quality of the dialogue clearly contrasts with the narrative prelude of lines 1 to 14:

> In Cloe's chamber, she and I
> Together sat, no creature nigh:
> The time and place conspired to move
> A longing for the joys of love.
> I sighed and kissed, and pressed her hand;
> Did all—to make her understand.
> She, pretty, tender-hearted creature,
> Obeyed the dictates of good-nature,
> As far as modesty would let her.
> A melting virgin seldom speaks
> But with her breasts, and eyes, and cheeks:
> Nor was it hard from these to find
> That Cloe had—almost a mind.
> Thus far, twas well; but to proceed,
> What should I do?—Grow bold.—I did.—
> At last she faltered, 'What would'st have?'—
> 'Your love,' said I, 'or else my grave.'—
> 'Suppose it were the first,' quoth she,
> 'Could you forever constant be?'
> 'Forever? Cloe, by those eyes,
> Those bubbies, which so fall and rise,
> By all that's soft, and all that's fair,
> By your whole sacred self, I swear,
> Your fondest wishes ne'er shall crave
> So constant, so complete a slave!'
> 'Damon, you know too well the art,'
> She sighing said, 'to reach my heart!'
> Yet oh! I can't, I won't comply.—
> Why will you press? Dear Damon why?'

The generic hybridity of narrative and dialogical verse in iambic pentameters is further emphasized when the speaker's dialogue on whether they will indulge in the "joys of love" breaks off abruptly and is ended by a number of suggestive asterisks behind which the probable result of the speaker's attempted persuasion is concealed.

The asterisks are followed by another narrative section that puts the whole poem into a different temporal framework of the past. By now, however, the speaker has put this burlesque episode on paper, and poetically recounts the story when he is being interrupted by Cloe, who finds the text. Intent on supposedly preserving her (lost) virtue by means of secrecy, she throws this incriminating document into the fire in order to erase any evidence of the story altogether.

> For Cloe coming in one day,
> As on my desk the copy lay,
> 'What means this rhyming fool?' she cries:
> 'Why some folks may believe these lies!'
> So on the fire she threw the sheet.
> I burned my hand—to save this bit.

Evidently, the speaker was reading his poetical production when Cloe entered the room, interrupted his reading, and refused a possibly incriminating ending to the reader. It is thus Cloe who interferes with the poet's authority by physically destroying part of the manuscript— thereby turning the poem into a fragment. Structurally, however, the dialogue is embedded into two parts, each of which asserts the author's ability to present the text to his readers, yet without the clear intention of revealing whether he enjoyed the pleasures of love. The final phrase —"to save this bit"—reveals the importance the speaker attaches to the preservation of the document, by then only a fragment of the narrative that is skillfully structured to accommodate the mode of the unfinished.

SATIRIC FRAGMENTS

Intermodal "cooperation" of one mode with another can frequently be found in fragment compositions; in fact, most fragmentary productions rely on such intermodal relations, and the more prominently the mode of the fragmentary occurs within the poem, the more fully realized is the fragment as a kind. The generic interrelationship between the fragmentary and satire testifies to a fruitful "cooperation," especially at the beginning of the century. A case in point is Thomas Warton the elder's "A Fragment of a Satire."[69] Warton (1688–1745), the father of the ode writers, Thomas and Joseph, apparently considered the implications of the fragment particularly suited to the discursive and digressive character of satire.[70] Although, formally, Warton uses the smooth and closed heroic couplet, as well as a stanzaic structure, the title of "fragment" may be explained by the author's perception that his defense of poetry is only one of the numerous statements that, like the allegory of *The Pilgrim's Progress*, could be continued, further elaborated on, or added to in time. The structure of the fragment is conclusive and closed; it forms an entity both semantically and structurally. At its center, Warton uses anaphoras to make his point about the degeneration of poetic standards:

> No more I rove collecting classic sweets,
> Nor warlike Homer's well-fought battles warm,
> No more I weep while awful Tragedy
> Like Sophocles array'd comes stalking by
> (Leading ill-fated Oedipus the Blind,
> Or the lame wretch in desert drear confin'd),
> Nor in mild Maro's groves and grots rejoice,
> Nor Doric Shepherd's sweetly-simple voice,
> No more convey'd by Pindar's rapid song,
> I see great Theron's car victorious whirl along,
> Nor crown'd with grapes with gay Anacreon laid
> Beneath a plantane praise some beauteous maid,
> But oft resounding in my trembling ear,
> Me thinks my country's dying groans I hear.

Warton's fragment may be understood in the context of a satirical impromptu that is spoken without further reflection, thereby faking spontaneity and linguistic immediacy. This aspect of extemporaneous composition and the lack of premeditation, however, are in stark contrast to the polished form and the stylistic devices used by the author. The anaphoric structure, the poem's rhythm, as well as Warton's systematic mention of all those poetic predecessors whom, in the remainder of his fragment poem, he considers neglected and misunderstood at the time, reveal that Warton was making use of the fragment for reasons that are connected with the poetic freedom afforded by a form that did not have any rule-bound restrictions. Within the (semantically and formally) open form of the fragment, Warton can then censure early eighteenth-century poetic practice and justify the need for satire.

Anne Finch, the Countess of Winchilsea (1661–1720), a friend of Matthew Prior but best known for her "A Nocturnal Reverie," also produced a number of fragments. She composed a "Fragment at Tunbridge-Wells," which she published in *Miscellany Poems, on Several Occasions* (1713):

For He, that made, must new create us,
Ere Seneca, or Epictetus,
With all their serious Admonitions,
Can, for the Spleen, prove good Physicians.
The Heart's unruly Palpitation
Will not be laid by a Quotation;
Nor will the Spirits move the lighter
For the most celebrated Writer.
Sweats, Swoonings, and convulsive Motions
Will not be cur'd by Words, and Notions.
Then live, old Brown! with thy Chalybeats,
Which keep us from becoming Idiots.
At Tunbridge let us still be Drinking,
Though 'tis th'Antipodes to Thinking:
Such Hurry, whilst the Spirit's flying,
Such Stupefaction, when 'tis dying:
Yet these, and not sententious Papers,
Must brighten Life, and cure the Vapours, &c.[71]

The explicit contrast between "He, that made, must new create us" and the effects of the spleen in women, from the beginning of the poem sets the satirical tone of the fragment. This humorous piece negates the mere possibility that the philosophical wisdom of Seneca or Epictetus might prove helpful in the treatment of the Spleen, for "Sweats, Swoonings, and convulsive Motions / Will not be cur'd by Words, and Notions." Instead, the countess prefers drinking at Tunbridge; rather than drinking the chalybeate waters of the wells, however, she describes an effect of intoxication as the inevitable result of drinking (alcohol). Only in the "Stupefaction" of intoxication will she rid herself of the Spleen and "brighten Life, and cure the Vapours."

This amusing fragment favors the material and intoxicating effects of drink over the more "sententious Papers" of classical philosophers. The fragment almost reads like an advertisement for drink and testifies to the countess' relative independence of thought and her countering of the expectations of polite society in favor of the "medicinal" faculties of drink. The style of satire used here is later on in the century used successfully by Christopher Anstey in his *New Bath Guide*.

Thomas Gray also produced a humorous fragment of the type of Lady Winchilsea's, which couples the generic features of the ode with a light subject. While the status of the humorous and satiric fragment differs in tone from poems that use the fragmentary for its association with the Pindaric (m)ode, its versatility reflects the possibilities for the cross-fertilization of genres and modes in the eighteenth century. Gray's "Hymn to Ignorance. A Fragment" is supposed to have been composed before October 1742, shortly before the poet returned to his alma mater at Cambridge. Gray's hymn is imitative of the graveyard theme that he himself would help to popularize with his "Elegy." His hymn, however, is not merely addressed to an abstract quality, to a personification, but to a deity that Gray associates and identifies with Cambridge. The start of the poem, as well as its invocation of "gothic fanes and antiquated towers," is fairly conventional in that it gives voice to the poet's happiness to return to the "peaceful shade" of Cambridge University. The Gothic attributes he uses to characterize Cambridge are positive and do not possess anything of the gloom on which the Gothic novel would focus.

The satirical intention of the hymn, however, is revealed when he addresses the goddess of Ignorance as "soft salutary power!" whom "Prostrate with filial reverence I adore." Expressing his pleasure at returning to Cambridge, but, more important, to the domain of Ignorance, Gray asks:

> Oh say, successful dost thou still oppose
> Thy leader aegis 'gainst our ancient foes?
> Still stretch, tenacious of thy right divine,
> The massy sceptre o'er thy slumb'ring line?
> And dews Lethean through the land dispense
> To steep in slumbers each benighted sense?
>
> (13–18)

The "massy sceptre" is expressive of the power that Ignorance possesses over her subjects, the "slumb'ring line." Instead of the advancement of knowledge, research, and an indefatigable interest in the promotion of epistemological truth, Gray sees his friends and future colleagues as being the "slumb'ring line" whose presence he missed so much during his absence from Cambridge.

Gray's apostrophe to Ignorance is not reciprocated, though, since "she hears me not, but careless grown, / Lethargic nods upon her ebon throne." He realizes that he cannot awaken the deity whose influence he used to court before. The "force of years" has changed his personality as well as hers. Earlier on, she "rode triumphant o'er the vanquished world" but has now entered a stasis that not even the indolent poet can appreciate. It is only by means of his imagination that he can revive the past and be one of the devotees of Ignorance:

> —yet still to Fancy new,
> Her rapid wings the transient scene pursue,
> And bring the buried ages back to view.
>
> (33–35)

He is able to catch one final glimpse of the goddess he once adored:

> High on her car, behold the Grandam ride
> Like old Sesostris with barbaric pride;
> . . . a team of harness'd monarchs bend
>
> . . . .
>
> (36–38)

With the realization that the "times" when he used to delight in indolence and ignorance are "for ever lost," he also becomes aware that his own life has changed. The end of his adolescence, his time as a student at Cambridge, means a new beginning, a beginning that is characterized by voracious study and research. Yet, while Ignorance, the "Grandam," has left his life, she will enter the lives of numberless students who will then become her devotees. The asterisks at the end of the poem indicate that, while his invocation was one that reflected the past, it will yet, for others, become present when they enter Cambridge. Although he has lost the link with Ignorance, he can still remember and re-evoke the past, but he will never be able to piece together the fragments of the past into a reality of the present.

Intermodal cooperation is responsible for the formation of new genres; the Pindaric manner with its association of hymnal praise and invocation stands for a notion of antiquity that poets such as Gray and Collins explored in their odes. Both poets used the odic poem in terms of speech acts that are replicated—in fragmentary fashion—through the literalization of address in print. The shifting between direct speech and description, discourse and description, necessitated a dynamic that aims to imitate and convincingly construct spontaneity. Even while reading a purportedly spontaneous act of speech, the reader is aware of its contrivedness. The little consensus that existed regarding the definitional boundaries of the ode allowed poets to appropriate the Pindaric manner to their own ends. Bards, doomed to perish in a world that hailed the print revolution, attempt one last time to resuscitate a past of

F R A G M E N T,

Suppofed to have been written among the RUINS *of*
* TINMOUTH CASTLE *and* MONASTERY,
NORTHUMBERLAND.

* * * * * * * * * * * * * * * Lonely indeed!
'Tis *awful!* 'tis fuperbly *ruinous!*
How chang'd this *Scene!* * * * * * * * * * * *
In Lethean *Years* long, long elaps'd,
The fwift-wing'd *Bullet* of *Deftruction,*
Loud-lab'ring from the brazen *Cannon's Womb,*
Pierc'd hence with *Light'ning* Speed, the perv'ous *Air,*
And roar'd, re-ecchoed from yon murm'ring *Main,*
Death's thund'ring *Summons,* and fulphur'ous *Call.*

How level'd now the lofty *Battlements!*
The fky-topt *Towers* and rock-rear'd *Batteries!*
Impregnable to Military *Art!*
That ever and anon *Time* totters now,
And rufhes down with dread *Precipitation!*
* * * * * * * * * * * * * * * *

---

* TINMOUTH CASTLE, the *Remains* of which are now to be feen adjacent to the Mouth of the River *Tyne,* in *Comit. Northumb.* was, at the Suppreffion of *Monafteries,* in the Reign of *Henry* VIII. made a Place of *Defence* and *Fortification* againft Foreign *Invafions.*——It is fituated upon a very high Rock, inacceffible from the *Eaft* and *North,* and is every Way fo well adapted to the Purpofes of War, as fufficiently demonftrates the *Military Skill* of our *Anceftors.*

Un-

John Brand, "Fragment, Supposed to have been written among the Ruins of Tinmouth Castle and Monastery, Northumberland," in *A Collection of Poetical Essays* (Newcastle upon Tyne: printed by I. Thompson, 1765). Reproduced from a copy in the author's possession.

orality, while the speakers of hymnal odes are in search of a lost Eden and an authentic, inspired voice. The fragmentary is the mode through which these attempts at gaining outspoken identity are made. Poets render the sublime in proto-Burkean terms as vast and too comprehensive for expression, relying on metaphors of the fragmentary and ruinous, and frequently contextualize the incomplete or partial representation of enthusiastic response to the inability of man to achieve completion, perfection, and immortality. The paradox between the holistic view taken by early theoreticians of the sublime ode and their concession that any such ode should be rapturous and use transitions that are abrupt and represent divine "fire" is symptomatic for deliberately conceived poems using the fragmentary. This is visually encapsulated, as on the printed page of John Brand's fragment that ornately frames the text, which advertises itself as fragmentary. This chapter's preoccupation with the Pindaric lyric has engaged with strategies of fragmentation that are related to modes such as the sublime, the hymn, and satire. The next chapter aims to trace strategies of fragmentation in longer poetic works that adopt the epic impulse and the significance of orality to come to terms with the anxiety of failure so persistent in eighteenth-century poetry.

3

Inventing the Long-Poem

Poets of the Interregnum and early Restoration turned hopefully
to the epic, and then turned away again, after having found that
it would not do. The poets needed to invent forms of narrative
that were not epic; they had to contrive something suited to
their particular purposes. New epic was just not possible.
Milton, the one successful modern epic poet, had at the same
time done the genre in—even for his own future purposes.

—Margaret Anne Doody,
The Daring Muse: Augustan
Poetry Reconsidered

UNLIKE THE SONNET, THE EPIC WAS A FORM THAT HAD A LONG HISTORY,
stretching from classic writers such as Homer and Virgil to moderns
like Milton and Spenser. Epics such as *Beowulf* or Homer's *Iliad* were
produced in the tradition of oral poems, meant for recitation. The oral
epic, according to C. M. Bowra, "is the mature form of improvised lays."[1]
Improvisation favors the use of repetition, as well as a looser structure
than that of secondary epics like *Paradise Lost*. Bowra notes that the
oral, primary epic is characterized by a fragmentary structure since, as
with eighteenth-century "Beauties" anthologies, the reciting poet could
not "expect to recite his poem in its entirety. He must be prepared to select from it, to recite only a section which must be relatively complete in
itself and not require too much explanation for its understanding."[2]
Recitation, to the eighteenth-century critic, was too spontaneous a way
of "reading" the epic, as it relied on a re-enacting of the poem's history,
as well as an emphasizing of those sections deemed sublime or heroic
that could be recited dramatically. It was also counteracted by the rise
of privacy. A heroic, public poem, therefore, contextually jarred with a
performative reading in an environment of privacy. Selection—although permissible in anthologies and miscellanies—was not in tune

with the holistic view that neoclassical critics of the epic preferred to take. The holistic approach to the epic had necessitated scholars to re-read classical principles of unity, realizing that the modern epic in various ways did not subscribe to these notions of unity. The realization of the difference between classical and modern epic practice culminated in the articulation of ideas of (mainly semantic) unity that could accommodate the difference without censuring it on the basis of the rules of classical epic.

This chapter offers a brief consideration of the epic and relates the development of the discontinuous long-poem in the eighteenth century to the decline of classical epic. It will be argued that the fragmentary mode frequently used by the epic enables the long-poem to foreground not the narrative, but the fragmentary and subjective, and that it expands the strategies of the Pindaric mode outlined in the previous chapter. The unity that was defined by classical theoreticians of the genre, reasserted by the French classicists and ultimately rejected by writers of the long-poem, becomes one of the defining marks—through its absence—of the fragmentary mode of the long-poem.

In sixteenth- and seventeenth-century England, poets and readers alike were aware of the post-medieval "burden of the past"[3]—that is, the literary heritage of previous generations. Since the epic as a genre was only used successfully (albeit appropriated to a number of changes that the genre had undergone since Homer) by such moderns as Spenser and Milton, it was no longer considered an appropriate medium to provide, construct, or represent the order and structure that were so highly valued within English culture at the time. Sir William Davenant's (1606–68) preface to *Gondibert* (1651), in that respect, is expressive of the need that he felt for appropriating the "heroic" to rules that were not classically legitimized:

> I cannot discerne by any help from reading, or learned men, (who have been to me the best and briefest Indexes of Books) that any Nation hath in representment of great actions (either by *Heroicks* or *Dramaticks*) digested Story into so pleasant and instructive a method as the English by their *Drama*: and by that regular species (though narratively and not in Dialogue) I have drawn the body of an Heroick Poem: In which I did not only observe the Symmetry (proportioning five bookes to five *Acts*, and *Canto's* to *Scenes* (the Scenes, having their number ever govern'd by occasion) but all the *shadowings, happy strokes, secret graces,* and even the *drapery* (which together make the second beauty) I have (I hope) ex-

actly follow'd: and those compositions of second beauty, I observe in the *Drama* to be the underwalks, interweaving, or correspondence of lesser designe in *Scenes*, not the great motion of the maine plot, or coherence of the *Acts*.[4]

The lack of "symmetry" is further emphasized by the formal incompleteness of the poem. And, as with other epic poems, the unfinished *Gondibert* attracted sequels or pieces that pretended to be hitherto unpublished parts of the epic. In 1685, therefore, *The Seventh and Last Canto of the Third Book of 'Gondibert', never yet printed* was published.[5] Davenant's text represents the problem that seventeenth- and eighteenth-century poets—with the aspiration to write epic—encountered. The epic was recognized as the most sublime kind, but any attempt at producing an epic had to negotiate the fragmentary that had been identified in Spenser and Milton but that a truly neoclassical composition, with its implicit ruling principles of harmony and (formal) "correctness," could not endorse. The result of this recognition was a search for a new poetic medium in which epic elements could be reworked, and two forms were singled out: the Pindaric ode and the long-poem.

An added difficulty that writers of secondary epic encountered was the changed context of literary production. While primary epics were the products of a culture of orality, eighteenth-century attempts at writing epic were conceptualized in a framework of scripturality. The classical epic poet relied on preformulated clichés that he combined performatively. Primary epic, therefore, depended on the repetition of formulae that had been memorized. Walter J. Ong argues that "memory played a quite different role in oral culture" and that the "entire language of the Homeric poems, with its curious mix of early and late Aeolic and Ionic peculiarities, was best explained not as an overlaying of several texts but as a language generated over the years by epic poets using old set expressions which they preserved and/or reworked largely for metrical purposes."[6] Translating the epic from a product of orality to a construct of scripturality entailed the emulation of heroic theme and, to a lesser degree, the fragmentary manner that in an oral culture would have been smoothed over by means of recital.

THE DESTABILIZED EPIC

Abraham Cowley (1618–67), a friend of Davenant's, aimed to produce a regular Virgilian epic; he also engaged actively in the popularization of the ode as a genre of writing that utilized the associations of the fragmentary. Samuel Johnson uses his attempt at epic—the *Davideis* (1656)—in his dictionary definition of the fragment. E. M. W. Tillyard describes Cowley's poem in the following words:

> As we have it, the *Davideis* is a fragment; four books out of the twelve which Cowley in his preface said he projected in imitation of Virgil. The whole action would have comprised the history of David, as told in the Bible, from a lull in Saul's hostility to him till the death of Jonathan at the battle of Gilboa.[7]

According to Tillyard, Cowley's production is "the first regular neo-classic epic in English on the Virgilian plan,"[8] produced not in stanza form but using the heroic couplet. The couplet, however, imposed a restraint with which the author could not appropriately cope; and, although "he adopts the form of the neo-classic epic," Tillyard notes, "he lacks the architectonic grasp that gives reason to the form"[9]: "Episode follows episode with no organic continuity."[10] The invocation at the beginning of Book 1,

> I SING the *Man* who *Judahs Scepter* bore
> In that right hand which held the *Crook* before;
> Who from best *Poet*, best of *Kings* did grow,
> The two chief *gifts* Heav'n could on *Man* bestow,[11]

introduces the epic convention of the poet's objective to "sing" the exploits, adventures, and trials of the hero. Cowley, Timothy Dykstal has pointed out, in the *Davideis* made an attempt at "epic revision."[12] It was his objective to "Christianize"[13] epic conventions, to demythologize the classical machinery, and to perfect—in Christian terms—what the pagan epic had lacked, an intention that he expresses in the preface to the *Davideis*:

> Amongst all holy and consecrated things which the Devil ever stole [and] alienated from the service of the *Deity*; as *Altars, Temples, Sacrifices, Prayers*, and the like; there is none that he so universally, and so long ursurpt, as *Poetry*. It is time to recover it out of the *Tyrants* hands, and to restore it to the *Kingdom* of *God*, who is the *Father* of it.[14]

This effort to "recover" and "restore" the highest form of poetry and to make it a Christian genre culminates in failure, as the projected further books were never written, possibly in the awareness that Cowley's vi-

sion of the epic was not negotiating the requirements and "general temper" of his own age with the "temper" of the biblical account of David,
the former of which E. M. W. Tillyard considered one of the essential
functions of the epic.[15] Dykstal holds Cowley's "hesitancy to assert classical (and pagan) ideals against the values of his often-conflicting Christian rationalism"[16] responsible for the "failure" of the poem. In other
words, "Cowley clearly means to differentiate between classical myth
and Christian truth, but he actually blurs the line between the two."[17]
The failure of Cowley's epic is therefore thematic—in that he did not
succeed in synthesizing myth, religion, and the seventeenth-century rationalism inspired by the New Science—and structural in that he realized that beyond the four books published he could not proceed structurally.

     Through his use of the dominant heroic couplet, Cowley formally
anticipates Pope's repeated attempts at producing an epic poem in couplets, while at the same time demonstrating that the closure of the couplet makes it an inappropriate metrical unit for the epic. Cowley's inability to work within the confining structural unit of the heroic couplet
may thus have been another reason for his publishing his *Davideis* as an
unfinished poem; his failure to achieve closure also indicates that, while
writers of secondary epic were looking for new structures in which they
could develop the epic narrative, they did not succeed in appropriating
it to such fashionable forms as the couplet or the quatrain stanza, which,
of course, had not existed in antiquity. Cowley's success as a writer of
odes, as a poet who throughout the history of the ode would be associated with the genre, testifies to his recognition that the fragmentary that
was objectionable in the epic could be used to advantage in the greater
ode. His notion of the Pindaric mode is equally applicable to the fragmentary genres of the eighteenth century, for they translated the "rage"
and "violent course" of the "Pindaric Pegasus" into structures that are
discontinuous, open, and fragmentary.[18] Cowley notes that, in the Pindaric mode, the

> *Numbers* are various and irregular, and sometimes (especially some of the
> long ones) seem harsh and uncouth, if the just measures and cadencies
> be not observed in the *Pronunciation*. So that almost all their *Sweetness* and
> *Numerosity* (which is to be found, if I mistake not, in the roughest, if
> rightly repeated) lies in a manner wholly at the *Mercy* of the *Reader*.[19]

Cowley's statement can be related to the oral epic, its performative nature, and the inevitable fragmentary effect in a presentation that relies

on improvisation rather than preconceived, organized, and planned poetic structures that do not require intonation and acoustic "sweetness."

Elegance, one of Johnson's measures of good style, is elevated to a poetic ideal that critics such as Percival Stockdale associated with the "elegant model of *Grecian* art."[20] Spenser, according to Stockdale (1736–1811), lacks this elegance, since he does not adhere to an Aristotelian understanding of unity and because he used poetic allegory. Allegorical poetry, according to Stockdale:

> could only be in vogue in barbarous times; for it is destructive of the very essence of true poetry; it is continually presenting to the reader monstrous impossibilities; it is continually giving persons, and exploits to the moral qualities of the heart, and mind; it is continually involving us in an intricate labyrinth of types, emblems, and mysteries; and thus it is for ever defeating the great ends of all genuine poetry, which are, as immediately, as instantaneously, as fire from heaven, to strike; to charm; and to captivate.[21]

Stockdale cites Dryden's censure of Tasso for his lack of plan and organization, and then extends his criticism to Spenser, whom he blames for his failure to achieve "uniformity."[22] He describes Spenser's technique of creating a sense of unity as an attempt at "combin[ing] his whole story by the person of *Arthur*" or "to leave a tale unfinished; and to throw the remainder of it into some remote canto."[23]

While Stockdale clearly evaluates Spenser's epic by means of criteria that were formulated by classical poets and critics, Richard Hurd (1720–1808), a friend of Thomas Gray and William Mason, and Bishop of Worcester, at the start of "Letter VIII" of *Letters on Chivalry and Romance*, articulates his intention of using a different approach to understanding Spenser's sense of unity, indirectly using the rhetoric of the fragmentary by adopting the architectural metaphor of the Gothic to characterize *The Faerie Queene*: "I spoke of criticising Spenser's poem under the idea, not of a classical, but Gothic composition."[24] Hurd is aware that the general plan of *The Faerie Queene* has appeared as "indefensible" to "classical readers" and that the apparent "disorder" of the poem's structure and method has frequently been the subject of criticism.[25] He compares Spenser's composition to a piece of Gothic architecture:

> When an architect examines a Gothic structure by Grecian rules, he finds nothing but deformity. But the Gothic architecture has its own

rules, by which when it comes to be examined, it is seen to have its
merit, as well as the Grecian. The question is not, which of the two is
conducted in the simplest or truest taste: but, whether there be not
sense and design in both, when scrutinized by the laws on which each is
projected.[26]

Hurd argues that Gothic art possesses "unity and simplicity, which results from its nature," and he continues that "in some reasonable sense
or other, it is agreed, every work of art must be *one*, the very idea of a
work requiring it."[27] In Hurd's critique of the text, he insists that any
composition is characterized by a sense of wholeness, if only thematic.
He defines the unified structure of *The Faerie Queene* by arguing that the
unity of the poem "consists in the relation of its several adventures to
one common original, the appointment of the *Fairy Queen*."[28] This unity,
then, "result[s]" from the "design, by which his subject was connected."[29] Patrick J. Cook offers yet another approach to the unity of Spenser's poem and epic generally by noting that the "artistic form adjusted
to the values of an increasingly human-centred, self-fashioning age" and
that, for that reason, Spenser's text was not so much characterized by
Aristotelian unity as by "the unity of the individual life."[30]

In contrast to *The Faerie Queene*, *Paradise Lost* is comprehended as the
last successful epic before Pope's attempt at translating classical Greek
epic. It is expressive of Milton's "paradisal longing," a longing that
would be more forcefully expressed in the "pervasive longing of the Romantics."[31] *Paradise Lost*, as Cook observes, represents Milton's "elaborate re-deployments of generic concepts."[32] Unlike Cowley, Milton could
not "write in a medium that imposed a restraint on the ardour that was
proper to him."[33] He counteracted the idea that "epic demanded the
added dignity of rhyme" and, for that reason, chose blank verse, which
did not imply the "kind of finality"[34] represented by rhyme, and the
heroic couplet in particular.

Its explicit intertextual reference is to the Holy Scriptures and, in
particular, to Satan's temptation of Eve and the ensuing original fall.
Milton turns the Paradise story into twelve books in which he describes
the progress of man from obedient servant of God to the willful representative of humankind who is capable of taking decisions and confi-
dent to stray from the way of life that God had assigned to him. The last
book ends with the departure of Adam and Eve from the Garden of
Eden and the awareness that man will have to repair the loss of innocence that had conditioned this expulsion from Paradise. Although Mil-

ton conceptualized *Paradise Lost* as a poem that was divided into twelve books, he resists the definite closure that a statement on the future existence of mankind might have implied.

Instead, Milton introduces a glimpse of hope by alluding to the arrival of the Messiah. This open ending, as well as Milton's sequel or response, *Paradise Regained*, indicates that he was attracted to the implications of a less closed and more fragmentary form such as Cowley's *Davideis*. Unlike the *Davideis*, however, Milton's religious epic is formally successful, since it conveys a comprehensive vision of what Tillyard termed an "architectonic grasp," a sense of thematic closure of the religious history of mankind.

Along with Milton, the work of Tasso would exert a significant influence on those eighteenth-century authors writing in the epic tradition. Tasso, in his use of the epic mode, had already popularized a version of the epic that made use of his "principle of the unifying 'verisimilar.' "[35] According to Mindele Anne Treip, Tasso saw the "need to defend interpolated episode in romance epic against the strictures of Italian neoclassicism, with its emphasis on single plot-line."[36]

> The problem of causality or logical narrative sequence, or in Tasso's words 'the connection of parts', becomes particularly interesting in this context . . . .Aristotelian theory of plot requires above all a certain inevitability in events: consequences must spring from causes, however trivial or overlooked these may have been. In Aristotle's ideal plot, as in nature, nothing is without a cause. Or to use Tasso's interesting formulation, "in nature there are no episodes." . . . Such a requirement is awkward for the romance-allegorical epic with its great variety of incident, multiple actions, and interpolated episode[s] often in a quite different mode. Appeals to the unifying ideal truth of the "verisimilar" are again the key to Tasso's defence of the mixed epic.[37]

It was on this defense of the "verisimilar" that Pope would found his own uses of the epic in his translations of Homer. Pope, however, apart from his efforts to translate original Greek epic, also tried to produce a British epic about Brutus, only a fragment of which, in blank verse, was completed:

> The Patient Chief, who lab'ring long, arriv'd
> On Britains Shore and brought with fav'ring Gods
> Arts Arms and Honour to her Ancient Sons:

> Daughter of Memory! from elder Time
> Recall; and me, with Britains Glory fir'd,
> Me, far from meaner Care or meaner Song,
> Snatch to the Holy Hill of Spotless Bay,
> My Countrys Poet, to record her Fame.[38]
>
> (1–8)

These initial eight lines were produced in 1743, one year before Pope's death, when the poet "was meditating an epic poem on civil and ecclesiastical government, whose hero was to be 'our Brutus from Troy'."[39] Even in these eight lines, a method of fragmentation that will be most prominently found in the compositions of mid-century writers of odes may be identified.[40] The first three lines deal with the "Patient Chief" Brutus, who "lab'ring long, arrived / On Britains Shore." A sudden transition is introduced in line 4 when Pope invokes the "Daughter of Memory," asking for the Muse's support and inspiration. The epic and invocative parts of the fragment of *Brutus* are more representative of the hymnal ode tradition than they are of traditional epic.[41]

It has been suggested in recent years that the decline of the epic and poets' inability to produce primary epic in the eighteenth century were partly due to the rationalistic enlightenment influence that was articulated in various genres of literature at the beginning of the century. What Dustin Griffin has termed the "loss of traditional epic machines and marvels"[42] is the eighteenth-century attempt to achieve objective truths that do not rely on the conventions of the marvelous and romance. Personification as a device would assume the importance that mythological "machines" had previously held, while the originally elaborate structure of the epic, for lack of heroic action and a leading hero, became more digressive and further developed the episodic character of the epic and its fragmentary implications in long-poems such as David Mallet's *The Excursion* (1728) or Richard Savage's *The Wanderer: A Vision* (1729). Pope's ambition to produce an epic on Brutus is an attempt to engage with the "temper" of his age — inspired by his involvement with the Patriot Opposition to Sir Robert Walpole — but also reflects his wish to continue and develop further the neoclassical traditions and ideals of the ancients. The rapport that Pope establishes with his own age is achieved by means of satire and the mock-heroic. Texts such as *The Rape of the Lock* (1712), in that regard, ought to be understood in this context of changing responses to the decline of the epic and the appropriation of new modes. Far from focusing on action and plot structure, Pope concentrated on making "narrative ride on a current of controlled energy,"[43] keeping action as "minimal" as possible. In that respect, *The Rape of the Lock* "proceeds in a series of tableaux, but without the surging energy that informs the epic."[44]

Apart from producing mock-heroic compositions that reworked the whole diversity of conventions of the epic, poets in the eighteenth century were seeking new directions in which they could develop their poetic creativity. Forms such as the heroic, pseudo-epic long-poems by Richard Blackmore (1654–1729) and Richard Glover (1712–85) were experimental but did not succeed in establishing a modal construction of the epic on a different plan that was used and further developed by other poets. Rather than considering the failed attempts at epic (which by that time represented most modern attempts at writing epic) as a discouraging element in their own endeavor to use aspects of the epic, they used features such as episodic and digressive narration for their own (descriptive) purposes and thereby created a new genre that, much more than the traditional epic, was characterized by its associations with a fragmentary mode.

Glover's *Leonidas* (1737) was read as a political epic, and early admirers frequently related it to the state of luxury in Britain at the time. In "To Mr. Glover. On his poem of Leonidas," Sir George Lyttleton praised Glover's "noble task" as a writer in favor of "Liberty and Virtue."[45] Lyttleton's poem voiced the general anti-Walpole stance against corruption, as well as the threat that Liberty was facing through Walpole's ever more prominent efforts to perpetuate his term in office. A second poem to Glover, by William Thompson, reproached Britons for their government's *laissez faire* attitude and the peace politics that Walpole pursued in order to delay action and war.[46] *Leonidas* was puffed by members of the Patriot Opposition in the opposition journals *The Champion* and *Common Sense* and was also centrally introduced by Henry Pemberton in his *Observations on Poetry, Especially the Epic: Occasioned by the late poem upon Leonidas* (1738).

Pemberton's little-studied volume is an important contribution not only to the theorization of the epic in the first half of the eighteenth century but also to the ways in which the Patriot Opposition appropriated the epic—through a critic like Pemberton—to their own propaganda agenda. A short consideration of Pemberton's *Observations* will establish this point: The author reconsiders Aristotle's notion of the epic, arguing that the epic does not primarily rely on the fable but on the depiction of character to fulfill its function as "moral composition to represent the good and ill effects of different characters and passions."[47] Pemberton hails both epic and tragedy as ideal media to illustrate the authenticity of the passions and their didactic effects. The epic poet, to Pemberton, is superior to the historian, since "history [only] confines itself, to what is done or suffered by particular persons," whereas "poetry shews, what speeches and actions do probably, or of necessity agree to the characters of men."[48] Even in a historical poem, the poet can implicitly and allusively respond to concerns of the present and advocate patriot ideologies, as Richard Glover does in *Leonidas*. In fact, in the Preface to *Leonidas*, Glover states that, in writing his poem, he followed an agenda of advocating "disinterested public virtue," observing at the same time that "the fall of Leonidas and his brave companions, so meritorious to their country, and so glorious to themselves, has obtain'd such an high degree of veneration and applause from past ages."[49] Leonidas is seen as a patriot of honor and virtue who is not devoid of sensibility and follows the dictates that Lord Bolingbroke would define as characteristic of the patriot king. Pemberton's *Observations* focus on the character of Leonidas and the heroic virtues that he adheres to and notes that "the poet ought to make it his chief endeavour to open the human mind, and bring forth the secret springs of action, the various passions and sentiments of men, upon which depends their good or ill conduct in every condition of life."[50] As an epic hero, Leonidas is a role model capable of "forming a right judgment upon the temper and behaviour of those, with whom we have intercourse"; he bestows "knowledge of the world" and "prudence."[51]

Although Pemberton's *Observations* were produced only after *Leonidas* had been published, his work both describes and—more important—legitimizes the (patriot) epic theory underlying *Leonidas*. Thomson's *Britannia* and *Liberty* preceded *Observations* and articulated the ideological preoccupation with civic virtue that Pemberton considers so central to the epic; however, they still use the abstract allegorical mode that Glover would take care to avoid, focusing on the progress theme rather than the exploration of epic character. Unlike Thomson's *Liberty*, Glover's poem remained popular throughout the century and was reissued in expanded form, in a fifth edition, in 1770. The *Monthly Review* emphasized the importance of character that Pemberton had used as a unifying mechanism in his theory of the epic: "Mr. Glover, the ingenious Author of *Leonidas*, hath, in the present edition, not only corrected the poem throughout, and extended it from nine books to twelve, but hath also added several new characters; beside placing some of the old ones in new situations."[52] The *Critical Review*, while acknowledging the significance of character, also focused on "the episodes in Leonidas, which are extremely beautiful and sentimental, full of fine description, and elevated morality."[53] The reviewer further noted that the "judgment likewise of the epic poet deserves to be highly praised, when he chuses a subject likely to captivate the attentions of the nation to which his work is principally addressed. The exploits of Leonidas, and his countrymen, for the cause of liberty, though admired by Europe, are certainly with peculiar propriety held forth to the view of England, the freest country in the world."[54] The focus on the episodic and the descriptive that Glover introduces to centralize his main character was to develop more prominently in the long-poem of the later decades of the century.

John Ogilvie, in the preface to his long-poem, *Rona: A Poem. In Seven Books* (1777), makes a (by then) conventional statement when he admits the difficulty of working within the generic boundaries of the epic:

> The most difficult province of him who attempts a species of *epic* poetry, is that of introducing *great and diversified characters*. The author does not call the following an Epic Poem; because the same may be thought too contracted, the actors too inconsiderable, and the event (though decisive) of too little consequence to confer upon it so high a denomination. Yet it is conducted upon the laws of the Epopoea, not because the writer had the silly vanity of making an exertion which his subject may not appear to justify, but because his fable seemed naturally to prescribe this arrangement.[55]

Rona is a narrative poem—written on the model of David Mallet's *Amyntor and Theodora* (1747). It uses digressive passages of reflection and joins these with dramatic scenes. Ogilvie's statement that "his fable seemed naturally to prescribe this arrangement" is important, as it insists that he is adopting the mode that is most natural for his poem— and this mode, as has been demonstrated earlier, is inspired by the destabilized notion of seventeenth-century epic.

The best-known poet who reworked the destabilized epic impulse is James Thomson (1700–1748). He combined epic and Georgic modes, varying description and discourse and refining his "epic" project as one that described Nature and man's position both within the country environment of Horatian retirement and the urban, political, and social influences affecting this supposed idyll. The vision that Thomson articulates is one of fragmentariness in which different constituent elements of the social, political, and natural landscapes are disparate but nevertheless affect one another.

JAMES THOMSON'S *THE SEASONS*

While Pope was praised for his "power of harmony" and the smoothness of the couplet, Thomson's *The Seasons* (1730–44) — almost from its
first publication — was censured for its lack of "method."[56] Its incoherence, interpolated episodes, as well as unbalanced structure, are reflected in and owing to Thomson's numerous revisions.[57] For that reason, *The Seasons* (like most long-poems produced during the eighteenth
century) was not praised for its structure, but for its sublimity and de-
scriptiveness. It is the sublimity of poetic description that Thomson
mentions in the "Preface" to the second edition of *Winter: A Poem*
(1726). The nucleus of *The Seasons*, *Winter* was a devotional poem that
clearly centered on the hymnal addresses of Winter and Nature, combining these with descriptive passages on the destructive but nevertheless awe-inspiring forces of the season.

The speaker's encounter with externalized nature is repeatedly
translated into internalized reflections — a process that Winter encourages, as he induces the reader to seek refuge in the company of the classics that support him in his philosophical musings. The descriptive and
contemplative passages are interrupted by passages of address, apostrophizing Fancy to remove him from the horrors of Winter:

> Oh! Bear me then to high, embowering, Shades;
> To twilight Groves, and visionary Vales;
> To weeping Grottos, and to hoary Caves;
> Where Angel-Forms are seen, and Voices heard,
> Sigh'd in low Whispers, that abstract the Soul,
> From outward Sense, far into Worlds remote.
>
> (74–79)

These passages contribute to the dramatic effect of the hymnal apostrophes, especially as the speaker leaves off his two modes of describing
external nature and contemplating its relation to human existence by
seeking transcendence, a transcendental escape that Winter will ultimately enable him to effect. Above all, these passages interrupt the linear temporal progression of the arrival of Winter; the poet deliberately
procrastinates the narrative of the effects of the approaching Winter by
invoking the all-comprehending deity of creation, Nature:

> NATURE! great Parent! whose directing Hand
> Rolls round the Seasons of the changeful Year,
> How mighty! How majestick are thy Works!

With what a pleasing Dread they swell the Soul,
That sees, astonish'd! and, astonish'd sings!
You too, ye *Winds*! that now begin to blow,
With boisterous Sweep, I raise my Voice to you.

(143–49)

This invocation is at the ideational center of the poem, making it a piv-otal statement in *Winter* and providing evidence for scholars who inter-pret Thomson as a poet in the tradition of eighteenth-century deism. The sublime that John Dennis had theorized in *The Grounds of Criticism in Poetry* is used as a defining mark of the powers of Nature and God, the latter of whom is addressed as "Father of Light, and Life." Dennis considered enthusiasm one of the essential characteristics of sublime address and observed that "Poetry was a Language which they [the poets] reserv'd for their Gods, and for the Things which related to them."[58] The apostrophes that Thomson integrates in *Winter* are expres-sive of his desire to establish a rapport with the divine, a rapport that is voiced by means of enthusiastic rhapsody. Thomson's dramatic concep-tualization of the sublime forces of Winter on both the environment and man further adds to the pseudo-mythological reading of Winter as a deity.[59]

In the revisions of the individual seasons the focus on the divine qualities of Nature is diluted, and they do not feature as centrally and strikingly as they do in *Winter*. Rather, as John Chalker has argued, the poet sets up a framework of opposition in which he juxtaposes the indi-vidual seasons.[60] By the time the seasons were integrated in the first edi-tion of *The Seasons* (1730), Thomson had realized that he had to provide more explicit structural pointers than merely rely on the sequential and chronological progress of the seasons in the year. The 1730 variant state of *Winter*, therefore, is preceded by an "Argument" that Thomson adds to assist the reader in identifying the overall progress of the poem.

The digressive and fragmentary form he chooses for the poem is well suited to expressing "poetical Enthusiasm, . . . philosophical Reflection, and the moral sentiment."[61] On the basis of his appreciation of the poet's descriptions, even the severe Samuel Johnson has difficulty in rejecting *The Seasons* and is willing to justify Thomson's digressions:

The great defect of *The Seasons* is want of method; but for this I know not that there was a remedy. Of many appearances subsisting all at once, no rule can be given why one should be mentioned before an-other; yet the memory wants the help of order, and the curiosity is not excited by suspense or expectation.[62]

Although Thomson used neoclassical poetic diction in *The Seasons*, he did not manage to create a structure that followed the Aristotelian notion of (dramatic) unity. In Ralph Cohen's words, "the unity of *The Seasons* constituted a serious puzzle for critics because it lacked the types of dramatic or epic unity which they had traditionally associated with poetry."[63] Robert Shiels, one of the earliest critics of *The Seasons*, writing of the unity and structure of the poem, observes that:

> the Four Seasons considered separately, each Season as a distinct poem has been judged defective in point of plan. There appears no particular design; the parts are not subservient to one another; nor is there any dependence or connection throughout.[64]

More than any other critic of Thomson, Shiels stresses the "defective" and "generically polymorphous"[65] character of *The Seasons*, considering digressions, elaborations on the natural beauty, order and man's part in the cycle of the seasons, as what Samuel Johnson, in Mallet's *The Excursion*, criticized as unnecessary diversions and a deviation from Aristotelian unity.[66] It is therefore to the design of *The Seasons* and other similar early eighteenth-century (long-) poems that Shiels and Johnson object. Earlier in the century, John Brightland had already censured poetic incongruity, insisting that the formal and generic success of a poem depended on a well-planned and executed design: "If a Design be necessary in the shortest and least of our Poems, it is vastly more necessary in those of greater length; which without this will infallibly prove intolerably tedious, and a rude indigestive Heap."[67]

The transitions and digressions to which Shiels refers in his commentary on Thomson's poem are expressive of a development in early eighteenth-century poetics—especially with regard to justifying epic fragmentariness—that favors a departure from the poetics of completeness and perfection to a more openly fragmented structure that uses thematic rather than structural unity as an organizing principle. These digressive episodes and sudden clear-cut transitions between different passages facilitate the editor's task when compiling a miscellany of extracts like a "Beauties" anthology.[68] James Sambrook, Thomson's modern editor, defends Thomson's work by pointing out that, despite the poet's digressions:

> the varied material of the poem is contained within a natural framework, so that all the minutely-observed weather signs and other natural features of the seasons, together with the seasonal activities of insects,

birds, animals, and men, are described in due order. . . . *The Seasons* also has some kind of unity of focus by its repeated glances at Milton.[69]

Sambrook does not acknowledge the fragmentary character of *The Seasons* but attempts to contextualize it in vague terms of a "natural framework" or its intertextual references to Milton or Virgil.[70] Others like John Aikin defended Thomson's "digressions" as "the overflowings of a tender benevolent heart,"[71] whilst it has also been argued that Thomson establishes a sense of hybrid unity by combining the features of the epic with those of the hymnal tradition.[72]

Oscar Kenshur identifies "a radical complication and, to an extent, transvaluation, of the relationship between fragmentation and unification, part and whole."[73] He argues that the fragmentariness of *The Seasons* is owing to Thomson's effacement and obliteration of distinction and differentiation, a process entailing "the conversion of variety into blank uniformity."[74] His argument is plausible when applied thematically to descriptions of night or fog, as Thomson in these descriptions indeed blurs the distinction between the objects represented in these settings. Kenshur identifies this "blending of discrete entities into a uniform whole" as "the opposite of order."[75] This "blending" overcomes hybridity and — through its violation of the individual components — creates fragmentariness, which is not the result of "epistemological fragmentation,"[76] as in the case of the Pindaric odes of Collins. He clearly opposes Ralph Cohen's view by stressing that Thomson's objective was to show the variety of nature within the harmony of the world, rather than presenting a unified vision of Nature:

> Both the poem and the world as we know it are discontinuous, consisting of a variety of parts that are radically distinct from one another. But just as the discontinuity of the world, as it turns out, constitutes an orderly differentiation of its parts, the discontinuity of the poem, with its arbitrary catalogue of natural objects, its didactic and narrative digressions, its tonal and generic variety, must be seen as representing not fragmentation but the order of differentiation.[77]

Kenshur's argument differs from mine in that he insists on Thomson's demonstration of an "order of differentiation," which he holds responsible for the fragmented *effect* of *The Seasons*. This view presumes an ideational design of the poem, rather than a structural one. My argument relies on the *structural* evidence that Thomson provides for the fragmentary *character* of the poem. The inter-generic use of the Pindaric mode in the hymnal invocations that the poet introduces are set off against the descriptive passages and digressions to create a dynamic poem with various foci, not necessarily as Kenshur insists, "proclaim-[ing] the glory of the whole."[78] The generic hybridity is more important than he is prepared to acknowledge, but it is through a combination rather than a synthesis—in the shape of "the order of differentiation"—that *The Seasons* becomes a dynamic and multifaceted poem that resists classification but that uses the mode of the fragmentary to achieve an interrelationship of what Earl Miner has termed "sense" and "descrip-tion." Miner argues that in the eighteenth century—following the desta-bilization of the epic—narrative is replaced by the modes of the discur-sive and the descriptive. The difficulty that poets had to negotiate was "that description and discourse required a proper relation,"[79] and it de-pended on the balance or imbalance of this relation in how far a text was regarded as fragmentary. This problem of unity or balance is ad-dressed in the preface to *Edge-Hill: A Poem* (1767), where Richard Jago (1715–81) notes:

> In the Execution of this Design, he endeavoured to make it as exten-sively interesting as he could, by the frequent Introduction of general Sentiments, and moral Reflections; and to enliven the descriptive Part by Digressions, and Episodes belonging to, or easily deducible from the Subject; divesting himself as much as possible of all Partiality in Matters of Public Nature, or Concernment; in private ones, following with more Freedom, the Sentiments, and Dictates of his own Mind.[80]

Part of the problem of what Kenshur terms the "discontinuous" form of *The Seasons* is the expected synthesis that the poet was to achieve be-tween *docere* and *delectare*. Thomson realized that a poem entirely dedi-cated to description would not be able to convey poetry's didactic func-tion. The rapport that he needed to establish with the reader was achieved through his more dramatic and lyrical passages. These pas-sages did not always achieve Earl Miner's ideal balance and harmony; rather, they were often distorted structurally by the transitions and con-nections that Thomson used to link discursive passages and description.

The fragmentariness of *The Seasons* is further reflected by Thomson's difficulty in introducing appropriate transitions. In that regard, the ma-jority of transitions that Thomson uses in *Spring* to connect different passages are introduced by a contrastive "but." Another possibility of opening a new section—though less frequent—is the conditional "if." Rhetorical questions can be part of the discursive invocations, while "then" denotes the consequence or effect of a process, or "thus" a demonstrative pointer given as a result of a lengthy digression. Rhetorical questions, too, are repeatedly introduced by "but." Yet, the contrastive function is not always fully realized, since in an accumulation of contrasts the conjunction loses its rhetorical and stylistic effect. Furthermore, "then" is introduced as an adverbial marker for a retrospect digression on the prelapsarian existence of man and nature, the age of eternal Spring, which is then contrasted again with the loss of innocence and corruption of the present. "Then" is frequently embedded in a "then . . . now" construction, which can also be introduced by "but." Other (not always effective) connectives include "hence," "since," "now . . . then," and "but now," as well as "yet." "Yet" is expressive of the contrast Thomson intends to establish to the preceding passage, but it also denotes simultaneity.

"Now" occurs in different functions in *Spring.* As in the poems of John Dyer and Collins, it need not always be used in its temporal meaning. It can be used in the sense of an interjection, which anticipates elliptically a later use: "Now, when the first foul torrent of the brooks, / Swelled with the vernal rains" denotes an incongruity between the present of the temporal "now" and the past tense "swelled." It therefore ought to be understood as an interjective statement that abruptly introduces a new passage, at the same time anticipating the following sentence: "now is the time, / While yet the dark-brown water aids the guile, / To tempt the trout."

Imperatives, which are, among others, used in the hymnal address, also introduce rhetorical questions:

> Behold yon breathing prospect bids the Muse
> Throw all her beauty forth. But who can paint
> Like Nature? Can imagination boast,
> Amid its gay creation, hues like this?
>
> (467–70)

Apart from this, Thomson uses "now . . . now" constructions to denote simultaneity. Contrasting discursive and descriptive passages, as John Chalker noted many years ago in relation to the theme of *The Seasons,* is one of the poet's central strategies. In a poem that is based primarily on juxtaposition and contrast, it is not easy to conceive how monotony or stylistic awkwardness could be avoided, as in a portion of text (714, 729) where the same connective conjunctions are used (supposedly constrastively) for two consecutive passages. Rather than providing an effective contrast, levels of priority are blurred and description is not subordinated to Miner's "sense."

The conjunctions that Thomson uses could effectively be employed in a shorter poem; the grammatical function of subordination is not always achieved when he opens new passages with temporal, conditional, or causal clause structures. The poet's dilemma, in that regard, consisted in his desire to approach the season from a multidimensional perspective that explored spring both spatially and temporally, as well as associatively. The lack of subordination of some parts to others is reflected in the imbalance between description and self-conscious address. Discourses exist next to each other but are not clearly related to each other. The hymnal elements, however, infuse the poem with a dynamism and dramatic effect that—despite the near-failure of connectives—establishes a unifying force that is also reflected in the sublimity commonly associated with the invocations in the odes of Collins.

In *The Excursion,* Mallet used a similar excessive repetition of identical transitions. Unlike Thomson, however, he only has one single hymnal invocation, at the opening of Book 1:

> Companion, of the muse, excursive power,
> IMAGINATION! at whose great command
> Arise unnumber'd images of things,
> Thy hourly offspring: *thou*, who canst at will
> People with air-born shapes the silent wood,
> And solitary vale, thy own domain,
> Where *Contemplation* haunts; O come invok'd,
> To waft me on thy many-tinctur'd wing,
> O'er Earth's extended space.[81]
>
> (1–9a)

Mallet does not aim to establish the sequential dialogue of Homeric epic, nor does he address a patron. Instead, he overpopulates his landscape with (at times, mythological, but mostly rhetorical) personifications and indulges in his excursive view of the universe. Due to the lack of interactive engagement with reader, patron, or deity and his focus on spatial exploration only, together with a strong fascination with the supernatural, *The Excursion* is even more structurally amorphous than *The Seasons*. *Spring* and *The Seasons* as a whole are held together by the interplay between the interactive aspect of apostrophe that echoes faintly Homer's "Godlike Race of Heroes,"[82] communicating with the gods and imploring them for success in battle. Mallet, aware of the structural "fault" of his poem, admitted in the "Advertisement" that his objective "was only to describe some of the *most* remarkable Appearances of Nature, [and that therefore] the Reader will not find in it that Unity, and Regularity of Design, which are essential in Epic and Dramatic Writings."[83] His focus clearly was on description and he therefore did not use the hymnal address in the ways that Thomson did. In the oral epic, the hymnal address had the important function of giving expression to the speaker's spontaneity, as well as the wish to overcome his (human) state of incompleteness by apostrophizing the deity.

By its very nature, the hymnal tradition is focused on the invocation, the celebration of the apostrophized in encomiastic terms (which usually is part of the invocation and then elaborated in the *pars epica*), as well as the petition that the deity is asked to grant. The instructive element of poetry that Thomson mentioned in the "Preface" to *Winter* is represented by the Georgic mode that he adopted from Virgil. Rather than writing a purely didactic poem in which there was no reason for a specific ordering of the ideas (as, according to Johnson, universal truth can be derived from the parts without being obscured by its structure), however, Thomson chose a number of discourses and modal elements that made the poem more varied but also more difficult to harmonize. Description, in that respect, is indirectly (judging by Johnson's focus on instruction in his "Life of Pope") understood as not very instructive, but mainly entertaining the imagination instead. Furthermore, while Pope in the *Essay on Criticism* (1711) was conceived of as intent on articulating generalities, Thomson in *The Seasons* aims to single out specific scenes and characters to confirm his universal "hymn" of the creation, a hymn that is concluded by the appended "Hymn to the Seasons."

Barbara Kiefer Lewalski's argument about "imaginative energy"[84] applied to rework the plurality of generic traditions is reflected in Thomson's choice to combine different modal qualities and, thereby, to create a novel genre: the descriptive long-poem. In this new kind of poem, none of the (lyric, epic, and dramatic) modes exists independently of the others, but they are interrelated in a way that creates action and progression. The conflation of the dramatic and the lyric is centrally acknowledged by Thomson's use of hymnal elements, a fact that explains why scholarship has repeatedly comprehended him as an early Romantic. The interactive uses of interjections, as well as temporal adverbs such as "Now" at the beginning of new paragraphs or semantic units, focus attention and serve as transitions, which in the context of the Pindaric ode were expected to be abrupt, as they reflected

sublime enthusiasm. The descriptive and digressive passages are derived from the epic; the action that usually characterized classical epic is
here introduced by means of lyric immediacy and invocations, as well as
the drama of such interpolated episodes as "Celadon and Amelia" in
Summer. The transformational and genre-synthesizing qualities that
characterize Thomson's long-poem make it possible to understand the
poem and its generic contexts, as well as the discourses, such as the
sublime, that the poet chooses.

One problem of critics dealing with the long-poem in the eighteenth
century has been their desire to interpret *The Seasons* in the contexts of
classical epic or Virgilian Georgic while, at the same time, applying the
Popean and Johnsonian category of "correctness." Thomson, generically, is closer to Milton and *Paradise Lost* than he is to Pope. Apart from
that, Thomson clearly derives inspiration from Milton's companion
pieces, "L'Allegro" and "Il Penseroso," two odes that adhere to the hymnal pattern. It is of central importance to recognize that the character of
Thomson's production not only is encomiastic but that it is also hymnal,
celebrating the divinity of the creation. As such, it is the product of an
inspired poet who articulates a rhapsody in terms that eighteenth-century critics such as John Dennis used to define the Pindaric ode. In his
long-poem Thomson succeeds in combining the two principal kinds of
the hierarchy of genres, the epic and the ode. He is the first successful
poet to use this "new" genre of fragmentation and thereby paves the
way for a more flexible and accepting appreciation of long-poems,
which, in the Romantic period, will no longer use the hymnal tradition
so central to *The Seasons* but will replace it with introspection, autobiog-
raphy, and a more prominent sense of immediacy.

Formally, irregularity in the long-poem was demonstrated not only
in the imbalance between "discursive" and "descriptive" passages; rather, the use of blank verse frequently counteracted the (inevitable)
structural closure and organization achieved by rhyme. Isaac Watts
notes that "the Design and Glory of Blank Verse" is "to avoid" "un-
pleasing Uniformity."[85] He insists on the "different Stops and Cadences
in Blank Verse" and warns against overpunctuation, which, Watts observes, can "reduce" "Verse too much into a Prosaick Form."[86] In *Conjectures on Original Composition*, Young, the author of the second most
popular long-poem in the century, explained that "what we mean by
blank verse, is verse unfallen, uncurst; verse reclaim'd, reinthron'd in
the true *language of the Gods*; who never thunder'd, nor suffer'd their
Homer to Thunder, in Rime."[87] He understood rhyme as a fall from in-

nocence and originality and recommended the "sweet, elegant, *Virgilian*, Prose"[88] of Addison: "What a fall it is from *Homer*'s numbers, free as air, lofty, and harmonious as the spheres, into childish shackles, and tinkling sounds."[89] The blank verse that Thomson used in his poem was recognized by Johnson as unique; no partisan of blank verse and experiencing "disgust"[90] at the blank verse of John Dyer, Johnson opined that Thomson's "is one of the works in which blank verse seems properly used. Thomson's wide expansion of general views, and his enumeration of circumstantial varieties, would have been obstructed and embarrassed by the frequent intersections of the sense, which are the necessary effects of rhyme."[91]

Young used blank verse in *Night Thoughts* and "was conscious of the rhapsodic lack of structure"[92] of his composition. *Night Thoughts* adopts the form of the anthology in that its composite structure is characterized by poems — "nights" — that, like Thomson's poems, rely on interpolated episodes, descriptive, and discursive passages, but that represent an ideational (if not structural) movement from incompletion and formlessness to completeness and fulfillment — death. In this regard, it is an attempt at overcoming poetically the fragmentariness of postlapsarian life and therefore concerned with the same identity-defining process as the hymnal odes discussed in the previous chapter. In this sense, Young's introduction in *Night* 1 of "Tired Nature's sweet restorer, balmy Sleep" prefigures the rest and finality of death that he anticipates with reflections on the pseudo-transcendent qualities of sleep.[93] An anonymous reader of *Night Thoughts* noted in "Over Young's Night Thoughts" that "Exalted by thy theme, we mount on high, / We spurn at earth, we claim our native sky."[94] Although Sleep can restore Nature, it is unable to soothe and restore the speaker whose sleep is characterized by "a sea of dreams / Tumultuous." The speaker considers Death as the ultimate source of repose, when he will no longer be haunted by nightmares and when rest will no longer be intermittent and temporary, but eternal. Young understands "sable Night" as a state that is akin to death in that it represents a complete and vacuous state of finality, "profound" darkness, and "dead" silence, as well as the seemingly supertemporal suspension from active terrestrial life. In *Night Thoughts*, Douglas Lane Patey notes, Young "advances a program of escape" "from all the entanglements of the self with its worldly roles."[95] His invocation of Silence and Darkness for assistance — assistance to taste the restoring sleep of Death — is conventional in that, once his petition is granted, he will have transcended human existence and entered the kingdom of the grave, a search for finality similarly expressed in Robert Blair's long-poem, *The Grave* (1743).

The dualism of the "double night"—the night as a symbol of primor-dial, pre-Enlightenment self and the night as a facilitator of the poet-speaker's contemplation—reflects the gulf between man and the in-spired poet, a gulf that can only be bridged by means of poetry. Douglas Lane Patey has remarked in this regard that the poet's task is one of creation and the "primary function of original composition is es-cape."[96] The poet's work reflects the "radical discontinuity between the temporal and the spiritual" but *Night Thoughts*—as a work inspired by the light of Night—induces the soul "to look inward, in order to disen-tangle itself from all merely worldly (and hence false) roles, and so to uncover its true self, whose home is in eternity."[97]

In revisiting the generic hybridity of *Paradise Lost*, both Thomson and Young attempted to synthesize modes in order to create a poem of new epic scope. Milton relied on action and progression through epic narra-tion in blank verse, at times interspersing the narrative with lyric state-ments by the speaker, thereby heightening the dramatic qualities of *Par-adise Lost*.[98] Thomson's (non-heroic) subject made it more difficult to rely on action as a unifying force, but instead introduced a variation of descriptive and discursive passages, passages of narration and contem-plation, that were supplemented by invocations of the deities or the ac-tion of interpolated episodes. He drew on the conventions of the hym-nal ode and thereby achieved the sublimity that mere description could not inspire. In *Night Thoughts*, the speaker's persona traces his thoughts, his mood changes, and his passionately expressed lament, thereby artic-ulating the sublime rapture that is characteristic of Milton but not, on the whole, of Thomson. For Young's speaker, each night is a stage plat-form from which he can declaim his feelings and the changeability of his passions and, what is more important, the changing tone of his re-flections. The dynamic between discourse and description that charac-terizes such long-poems as *The Seasons* and *Night Thoughts* is used as a backdrop in Glover's *Leonidas*, in which the hero's character features in a framework of episodes that are loosely connected by the action of the poem.

Glover's poem—owing primarily to its topicality—was one of the few successful heroic poems deploying the epic impulse in the eigh-teenth century. By the time it was published, poets no longer necessarily or exclusively focused on an heroic theme. The long-poem of the Thomsonian kind draws strength from classical texts such as Virgil's *Georgics* and accords a more central position to the voice of the poet, who no longer necessarily speaks as a man for mankind but as an individual uttering his subjectivity in a fashion that classical epic would not have permitted. The long-poem, as illustrated in this chapter, frequently adheres to the ideational search for completeness, representing man's attempt to overcome postlapsarian fragmentariness, and in this search uses the fragmentary as a self-conscious device of discourse and reflection, rather than linear progression and action. The orality/scripturality problem that prevented eighteenth-century poets from completing a primary, recitative epic, a poem of epic scope that relied on performative consumption, or a secondary epic tracing a religious story as successfully as Milton culminated in the fashioning of the generically hybrid form of the long-poem, which was frequently criticized for its lack of method but also as frequently commended for its descriptive powers and its potential to deal with the pressures of new poetic subjects.

4

"New" and "Authentic" Fragments

THE ESTABLISHING OF A LITERARY CANON OF "CLASSICS" IN THE EIGH-
teenth century not only resulted in editions of Milton, Spenser, and
Shakespeare, but also in appropriations and spin-offs of these poets'
works. Editors and compilers frequently included extracts from epic
poems such as the *Iliad*, *The Faerie Queene*, and *Paradise Lost* in "Beauties"
anthologies. The "amphibian status"[1] of these poems' structural makeup
lent itself to the inclusion in collections of the supposedly best parts of
these compositions, enabling readers to appreciate their "spirit" and
"manner," without having to trouble to read the works in their entirety.
Other modes of appropriating the epic and "primitive" poetry entailed
authors' providing "sequels" and "updates," thereby reinventing the
original text, as well as recontextualizing it. Booksellers published "Mil-
tonized" poems, which, at times, blurred the distinction between imitation and an ostensibly fragmentary (but hitherto unpublished) part of
Paradise Lost. Also, editions of *Paradise Lost* were produced that were not
only modernized in spelling but that had been paraphrased in prose to
avoid the difficult poetic blank verse of Milton.[2] So, in 1729, the first
French prose translation of *Paradise Lost* was produced, a translation
that was curiously rendered back into English by a "Gentleman of Oxford" in 1745:

> Another attempt, made in 1773, to render the poem intelligible to "per-
> sons of a common Education" was James Buchanan's "First Six Books
> of Milton's *Paradise Lost*, rendered into Grammatical Construction, the
> words of the Text being arranged, at the bottom of each Page, in the
> same natural Order with the Conceptions of the mind; and the Ellipsis
> properly supplied, without any Alteration in the Diction of the Poem."[3]

In this process of appropriation and fragmentation, the question of literary forgery was never explicitly raised, since it was evident that the

original text could still be consulted; it was clear that the "translated" or anthologized version was only to assist the reader in understanding the original. It must be remembered, however, that although there were a great many of these appropriations of traditionally canonical works, this method of appropriating them was not universally accepted as adequate (especially by serious Milton scholars); the "scholarly" Milton, as opposed to the "popular" Milton, was edited carefully, and textual commentaries on Milton were modeled on scriptural commentaries on the Bible, including heavy annotation.[4]

SPENSER AND FRAGMENT-IMITATION

One way of capitalizing on the canonicity of an author's work was to provide not an appropriation (that is, translation, paraphrase, or annotated edition), but an imitation or an "authenticated" fake. Gilbert West, the editor of Pindar's Olympian odes, claimed to have discovered a canto of Spenser's *The Faerie Queene*, which he published as *A Canto of the Fairy Queen* (1739).[5] In West's case, the poet, under the pretence of only editing the text, states that the canto was "Written by Spenser" and had "Never before [been] Published." Highly praised, this canto "enraptured and enmarvailed"[6] Thomas Gray; however, West's ploy to pass off his canto as Spenser's seems to have been obvious, as it did not trigger an authenticity debate of the kind that surrounded Thomas Chatterton's and James Macpherson's supposedly authenticated fakes. West's canto was republished by Robert Dodsley under the revised title of *The Abuse of Travelling. A Canto. In Imitation of Spenser.*[7] Once it had appeared in Dodsley's *Collection*, it was even more readily and widely available. In 1751, West published a second Spenserian imitation, *Education: a poem in two cantos. Written in imitation of the style and manner of Spenser's Fairy Queen*, of which only the first canto was ever published, however, thus making it a fragment of a supposed fragment.

Stylistically, West in his first canto uses the Spenserian stanza successfully, if with a slightly overly contrived irregularity in the pentameters. Furthermore, he uses devices such as grammatical inversion and anaphoras too prominently; at the same time, he fails to use the diverse allegory of Spenser. The first seven stanzas do not resemble *The Faerie Queene* at all, either in diction or in the poet's use of allegory. Stanza 8, however, provides a good attempt at a stanza that Spenser might have produced himself:

Forthy, false Archimago, traytor vile,
Who burnt 'gainst Fairy-land with ceaseless ire,
'Gan cast with foreign pleasures to beguile
Her faithful knight, and quench the heavenly fire
That did his virtuous bosom aye inspire
With zeal unfeigned for her service true,
And send him forth in chivalrous attire,
Arm'd at all points adventures to pursue,
And wreak upon her foes his vowed vengeance due.
(64–72)

West here embeds his canto into the semantic framework of the original, introducing the arch-fiend, Archimago, who tries to tempt the Knight of the Red-Cross. This stanza is followed by a further fifty stanzas that use Spenserian diction, which is explained through the annotation provided by West.

It is significant that the piece was published anonymously. This is self-explanatory, since the editor's name does not necessarily have to appear on the title page, unless the editor is involved in the annotation of the text and hopes to have his work acknowledged by a possible patron, for instance. Furthermore, since Spenser is affirmed as the author by the initial statement on the title page, there is no further question about the authenticity of the canto. Had the poem been convincing, however, it is likely that it would have been published by the Tonson business, which at that time owned the copyright for Spenser's works and would therefore undoubtedly have had a commercial interest in extending its copyright to unpublished material.

An earlier supposedly "original" canto by Samuel Croxall (1688/9–1752), alias Nestor Ironside (Steele's pen name), the translator of Ovid's *Metamorphoses*, makes a more explicit effort to prove the authenticity of the canto. At the beginning of his Preface, Croxall notes that "I am not insensible with what Reason the following Piece of Spencer will be suspected to be spurious, if a true and fair account not be given of it."[8] And he starts his anecdote by saying that "my Great Grand-father, Sir Caleb Ironside, was a School-fellow and intimate acquaintance of Mr. Spencer's . . . [and that] the Poet communicated all his Writings to Sir Caleb, before he made them Public."[9] How he came by it, is explained by the following:

Upon rummaging my Father's Study, after his Death . . . among other Family-Reliques, I found several Sonnets and Pastorals, written by Sir

Caleb. . . . From a dusty heap of this antiquated Poetry, I drew the following Canto, which I found a little disfigur'd with Interpolations and
Amendments, all seeming to be written by the same Hand. At the end of
it was written, in Sir Caleb's Hand; This is my dear Friend and School-
fellow, Munne Spencer's own Hand-wryting; but never imprinted, because not approved of by him, though I think it inferior to none of his
Allegories.[10]

Croxall skillfully explains the faulty character of the canto in that "several Parts of it seem to be written with an unusual Flatness, with a lan-
guid faint Spirit the Author at times was no Stranger to; and several of
the Alexandrines, at the Close of the Stanza's, were undoubtedly
breath'd out in the Height of a Phrenzy."[11] Concluding his preface,
Croxall insists, however, that "I must warn him [the reader] not to censure the present Fragment, unless he knows himself to be well ac-
quainted with Spencer, and his manner of writing,"[12] thereby assuming
the position of an editor who has researched the history of the text and
ascertained its genuineness.

Both Croxall and West imitate Spenserian mannerisms very closely,
"not merely in archaisms but also in his profusion of monosyllables and
his use of a loose, naïve syntax, which were at sharp variance with the
neoclassic search for the tight, closely-knit word order and compact,
weighty lines."[13] While West and other imitators of Spenser in the eighteenth century used *The Faerie Queene* as a point of reference to authenticate their works, by the mid-eighteenth century, literary appropriation
took a different line of development in that, through antiquarian inter-
ests, more attention was being paid to poetic forms that were not an integral part of eighteenth-century "high culture" poetics.

The success of West's and Croxall's imitative cantos was largely
due to their political topicality. Croxall's cantos "attack[ed] the Tory
minister [Robert] Harley's peace-making attempts with France and
Spain" and "were taken seriously enough by Harley's ministry to war-
rant a refutation of the first to which an entire issue of the Tory *Exam-
iner* was devoted."[14] By contrast, as Christine Gerrard has pointed out,
"West's Spenserian stanzas deal with the theme of the Grand Tour—a
double-edged tool, both rehearsing standard Opposition complaints
about the pernicious influence of foreign travel on the morals of 'Old
England', yet also operating as a focus for satirical critique."[15] Both
cantos are characterized by their skillful use of the Spenserian stanza.
The deployment of the stanza was the most direct reference to *The
Faerie Queene*, even though most eighteenth-century imitations of Spen-

ser focus on his manner rather than his allegory. Earl R. Wasserman notes that:

> in the first half of the eighteenth century the [Spenserian] stanza was inextricably bound up with the use of allegory and the imitation of Spenser's 'ludicrous' manner, and would have been considered inexcusable had it been employed for its own musical effects. But the repeated use of it in poems increasingly more remote from Spenser and the gradual decay of the closed couplet had established it as a worthy poetic form. No revolution had taken place in poetic taste; the stanza, which owed its survival to an interest in the *Faerie Queene* for other reasons, had crept slowly and subtly into a position of independent significance.[16]

John Hughes (1677–1720) was among the leading Spenser scholars of the eighteenth century and published his six-volume edition of Spenser's poetical works in 1715. He has been called the "greatest Spenser scholar of the early eighteenth century."[17] In his "Remarks on the Fairy Queen," he points out one feature that to poets such as West would appear like an invitation to produce their "original" cantos of *The Faerie Queene*; commenting on the unity of the poem, Hughes notes that the "several books appear rather like so many several poems than one entire fable; each of them has its peculiar knight and is independent of the rest; and though some of the persons make their appearance in different books, yet this has very little effect in connecting them."[18]

Since it was commonly assumed that some of the original cantos of Spenser's romance had been lost, Hughes is quick to find explanations for Spenser's lack of detail regarding the Arthurian legend. At the end of his essay, Hughes, for that reason, stresses that "I cannot think Spenser would wholly omit this [the Arthurian legend], but am apt to believe he had done it in some of the following books which were lost."[19] Hughes, without intending it, encouraged literary imitation in that interest shifted from the actual editing process of the existing text to versions and variants of the text that had not hitherto been published but that were "newly" discovered or invented. Also, Hughes engages with the fragmentary structure of *The Faerie Queene* by assuming that one of these "newly" discovered cantos could be integrated (without difficulty) into the otherwise fragmented makeup of the poem.

In his edition of *The Faerie Queene*, Hughes repeatedly argues that the incoherence and incompleteness of the text must not be seen as a defect; rather, the text should be considered as of "a particular kind" that was modeled on the Italian tradition of the epic and not on the ancients. He thereby foreshadows Richard Hurd's claims that Spenser's production ought to be understood against the background of a Gothic composition. Hughes does not draw any conclusion from the fact that *The Faerie Queene* is incomplete, that it is thus a fragment that consists of independent allegorical episodes that are, however, only loosely connected to each other. Joseph Addison, anticipating Hughes, had even termed the romance "one continued Series of [Fables] from the Beginning to the End of that admirable Work."[20] Hughes's edition and critical essays not only contributed to creating a taste for imitations and imaginative appropriations of Spenser's text, but they also further helped to popularize a generic conceptualization of the fragment that had been stigmatized in early eighteenth-century poetics.

While West pretended to have discovered a canto of *The Faerie Queene* that had hitherto been unnoticed, William Shenstone published the first version of his Spenserian imitation, *The School-Mistress*, as a burlesque in 1737. From the 1730s onward, poets such as Shenstone and Thomson showed a profound interest in the Spenserian heritage, and their attempts to imitate Spenser's romance were mainly made on the basis of an exact imitation of the Spenserian stanza, as well as of a burlesque theme. *The School-Mistress* and *The Castle of Indolence* undoubtedly are the best but certainly not the only successful imitations of Spenser's style.

In his last published poem, *The Castle of Indolence* (1748), Thomson admits his indebtedness to Spenser from the start. The Advertisement emphasizes that this "Poem being writ in the manner of Spenser, the obsolete words, and a simplicity of diction in some of the lines which borders on the ludicrous, were necessary to make the imitation more perfect."[21] Thomson implicitly introduces the conventional dialectic of perfection and imperfection. In that respect, had he attempted to rewrite Spenser's romance in the periphrastic (Miltonic) diction of the eighteenth century, his imitation would have been contextually imperfect. Instead, he hopes that he can partly dissolve the imperfection that an imitation like his inevitably entails. Bearing in mind, however, that *The Castle of Indolence* was originally planned as a private poem, as "little more than a few detached stanzas, in the way of raillery on himself, and on some of his friends"[22] and that John Armstrong (1708/9–79), the author of *The Art of Preserving Health* (1744) and a close friend of Thomson's, provided the final burlesque stanzas of the first canto, it is not surprising that the composition has retained some degree of fragmentariness.

According to Gerrard, the poem is not only "an allegory of the poet's mind"[23]; rather, Thomson in the figure of Archimage provides one of those figures of corruption and corrupting influence that feature in anti-Walpole writings of the 1730s. *The Castle of Indolence* therefore reverberates with the political concerns of corruption of the earlier decade, but it also advocates a sentimentalism in which the honor of a poet-knight is asserted by means of activity against a dishonest and dishonorable ensnarer of the people. Thomson's long-poem is still informed by the epic impulse; unlike in his two earlier poems, however, he appears to have realized that the usage of allegory of the kind deployed in *Britannia* and *Liberty* would not be effective for a supposed imitation of Spenser.

Thomson models the first canto on Spenser's episode in the Bower of Bliss. It is Archimage, the "wicked wizard," who—in stanza 27— lures people with his enchanting song in order to admit them to his fairy country of idleness:

> Thus easy robed, they to the fountain sped,
> That in the middle of the court up-threw
> A stream, high-spouting from its liquid bed,
> And falling back again in drizzly dew:
> There each deep draughts, as deep he thirsted, drew;
> It was a fountain of Nepenthe rare:
> Whence, as Dan Homer sings, huge pleasaunce grew,
> And sweet oblivion of vile earthly care,
> Fair gladsome waking thoughts, and joyous dreams more fair.

At the end of Canto 1, Thomson points out that the apparently idyllic setting of the garden of idleness is an illusion, for it does not give a purpose or direction to the "Sons of Idleness." Stanza 73 articulates Thomson's justification for interference with the wizard's doings, since:

> A place here was, deep, dreary, under ground;
> Where still our inmates, when unpleasing grown,
> Diseased, and loathsome, privily were thrown.
> Far from the light of heaven they languished there,
> Unpitied, uttering many a bitter groan,
> For of these wretches taken was no care:
> Fierce fiends and hags of hell their only nurses were.

The wizard's attempt to create a surrogate paradise, a paradise regained, has failed, and those who have outlived a life of idleness and pleasure are discarded underground in order for his illusory garden of happiness not to be disturbed. By imprisoning "these wretches," he further fragments the order of harmony and balance that had been destroyed with the original fall. The dungeon underground thus symbolizes the fragmentariness of postlapsarian life and at the same time stresses the need for a true bard to deliver these "wretches" from their confinement. Thomson takes as a starting point an episode from *The Faerie Queene*, but then develops his imitation into a composition on the (societal) importance of the truly inspired bard. He fragments the originally allegorical structure of Spenser's text and decontextualizes his production into a text that hardly follows Spenser's quest strategy.

Thomson reworked the epic impulse and used it to outline the progress of industry in the second canto. He combined pseudo-Spenserian diction with a notion of the epic that was classically inspired. This combination of modern with classical elements can be found in a large number of generically hybrid long-poems, which advertise themselves as imitations of "classics." A fascinating example of the complexity of generic experimentation was written by Michael Bruce (1746–67). A minor Scottish poet whose writings were profoundly inspired by his reading of Greek poetry, Bruce produced "The Musiad: A Minor Epic Poem. In the Manner of Homer. A Fragment," which was printed in his posthumous *Poems on Several Occasions* (1770). It is an interesting poem in a number of respects, but the title with its three generic terms deserves special attention. Bruce specifies his poem as a "minor epic poem." In fact, in this category it is related to *The Castle of Indolence* and *The School-Mistress*. Its subject is humorous, as the poet deals with the fall of Lambris, the mouse king, who had proven his valour many a time in stealing food from a farmer. The theft is seen as an heroic exploit, as illustrated in stanza 2:

> A farmer's house he nightly storm'd,
> (In vain were bolts, in vain were keys);
> The milk's fair surface he deform'd,
> And digg'd entrenchments in the cheese.
>
> (5–8)

Bruce in his mock-heroic production announces that he has used the "Manner of Homer" for his production, that it is imitative of the mode of Homer, a mode that vaguely echoes the Pindaric mode. The opening of the poem, in that respect, does not provide the usual invocatory address to the deity for support of the singer, but briefly introduces the mouse-king:

> In ancient times, ere traps were fram'd,
> Or cats in BRITAIN's Isle were known;
> A mouse, for pow'r and valour fam'd.
> Possess'd in peace the regal throne.
>
> (1–4)

It is only in stanza 14 that the poet reveals the king's name, and even then in a manner that appears deliberately belated, humorous, and mock-heroic:

> Thus LAMBRIS fell, who flourish'd long,
> (I half forgot to tell his name);
> But his renown lives in the song,
> And future times shall speak his fame.
>
> (53–65)

The title mention of Homer strikingly establishes the contrast between the heroic exploits of the *Iliad* and the charming valor of Lambris. When John Bancks observed that "the Subject of the Epic Poem must be grand and interesting, the Language elevated, and the principal Events of it marvellous,"[24] he clearly referred to the epic as a comprehensive account of the "temper" of the age; "The Musiad" lacks this elevated language or the use of the marvelous. The additional generic title reference to the fragment offers Bruce the opportunity of constructing his production as part of a larger whole, a whole that is imagined rather than actually extant. The poem's title qualifies the production in a number of ways and therefore—rather than creating a sense of accidental fragmentation—establishes a clear sense of the structuring, planning, and conceptualization that Bruce's poem has undergone.[25] The formal hybridity of "The Musiad" is related to that used in "Beauties" anthologies.

The anthologizing impulse enabled a level of generic complexity that was rarely achieved in a single poem. Thomas Warton, who had already edited the Oxford miscellany, *The Union*, was also responsible for the publication of *The Oxford Sausage* (1764). The latter contains "An Imitation of Spenser." The poem is a fragment that—through its title—establishes its connection explicitly with Spenser; yet, the main feature that reveals the author's intention of imitating Spenser is his use of the Spenserian stanza and the concluding alexandrine. Spenser's language, by the mid-eighteenth-century, was available in dictionaries and glossaries. The Spenserian fragment published in *The Oxford Sausage*, like Shenstone's imitation, adopts the character of burlesque. The anonymous author deals with a rather delicate domestic piece of pottery, the "Vase of sovraign use." The description of this chamber pot is clothed in Spenserian diction, as demonstrated in stanza 1:

> A Well-known Vase of sovraign Use I sing,
> Pleasing to Young and Old, and Jordan hight
> The lovely Queen, and eke the haughty King
> Snatch up this Vessel in the murky Night;
> Ne lives there poor, ne lives there wealthy Wight,
> But uses it in mantle brown or green;
> Sometimes it stands array'd in glossy white;
> And eft in mighty Dortours may be seen
>   Of China's fragile Earth, with azure Flowrets sheen.[26]
>   (1–9)

This imitative fragment of Spenser is representative of a trend either to modernize, revise, or develop fragments in the style of one of the primitive geniuses of Britain. Joseph Sterling (fl. 1765–94), the leading Irish Spenserian of his generation, who also produced Icelandic odes and an epic on Richard Coeur de Lion, in the Advertisement to his collection of *Poems* (1782), notes:

> The ingenious Mr Warton, in the first volume and fifteenth section of his History of English Poetry, speaks of the story of CAMBUSCAN in terms of the highest respect. He says, that after the KNIGHT'S TALE, it is the noblest of the productions of Chaucer: he proves that it is an Arabian fiction, engrafted on Gothic chivalry. This poem was continued by Spenser, and admired by Milton. It has been considerably improved by Mr. BOYSE, the Modernizer. The Concluder feels his poetic powers far inferior to those of CHAUCER and SPENSER.[27]

Sterling traces the process of translation and "improvement" that a fragmentary text such as "Cambuscan" undergoes and testifies to the variety of possibilities of appropriation offered by the fragmentary. In the Advertisement, he shows why Chaucer's Middle English production appealed to medievalists like Thomas Warton. Much more than the "Arabian fiction" and the "Gothic chivalry," Sterling is interested in what earlier poets such as Spenser and Boyse have done with Chaucer's text. The "Concluder," therefore, continues a process of improvement that Spenser had started, a process that aimed to appropriate "Cambuscan" to the courtly taste of the Elizabethan period. Boyse then corrected the text by rewriting the meter and textual structure, trying to eliminate the primitive medieval character of the composition, while Sterling further decontextualizes the text and rewrites it as a composition that has now become an independent text, no longer part of the *Canterbury Tales*.

The Reverend Christopher Pitt's (1699–1748) "The Art of Preaching, A Fragment. In Imitation of Horace's Art of Poetry" was published in Warton's *The Oxford Sausage*, too.[28] Pitt was a well-known translator, and at the age of 20 produced a metrical version of Lucan's *Pharsalia*, which he presented to the examiners for election at New College. He published the *Art of Poetry* in 1725 and translated Virgil's *Aeneid* into heroic couplets in 1736. The fragment in *The Oxford Sausage* lacks the systematic organization of Horace's treatise in that the author provides digressive examples of sermons, commenting on the appropriateness of subject matter and the suitability for those to whom sermons are being preached. What Pitt aims to do is to provide practical advice such as the following:

> Some easy Subject chuse, within your Power,
> Or you will ne'er hold out for Half an Hour.
> ·
> Begin with Care, nor, like that Curate vile,
> Set out in this high prancing stumbling Style:
> ·
> Ye country Vicars, when you preach in Town
> A Turn at Paul's, to pray your journey down,
> If you would shun the Sneer of every Prig,
> Lay by the little Band, and rusty Wig:

"The Art of Preaching" resolves itself in commonplaces without actually providing a helpful guide to the modes or the structure of preaching. Instead, the examples of a moderate style that promotes religion in a simple and convincing way are chosen to illustrate that the author does not consider his production a truly intellectual exercise but that, on the contrary, he takes it to be an unfinished work in progress that will be completed and perfected by each preacher's personal experience — hence the asterisks at the end of the poem indicate that the author's reflections end there but that the theme may be more comprehensively and systematically developed further by the reader himself. "The Art of Preaching" presupposes reader engagement with the text in the sense that the text is being created out of fragmentary segments of meaning that are combined performatively through oratory.

"PRIMITIVE" POETRY AND THE FRAGMENTARY

The engagement with the cultural and national past became central not only to ruin poetry but also to poets (re)inventing a past to articulate a statement on the Union of Kingdoms. This modified interest in the past is reflected in an aesthetic shift of emphasis from the exclusive model of antiquity to ideals that derived from medieval (vernacular) literature. Not only were Chaucer's *Canterbury Tales* read again, but Thomas Warton in his *History of English Poetry* even dedicated an entire literary-historical work to the study of the literature of the Middle Ages. Apart from that, Lady Elizabeth Halket Wardlaw produced a fragment of a supposedly ancient Scottish epic, Thomas Gray "translated" Old Norse poetry ("The Fatal Sisters" and "The Descent of Odin"), Thomas Percy collected and "corrected" literary "reliques," and James Macpherson published *Fragments of Ancient Poetry*.

Lady Elizabeth Halket Wardlow (1677–1727) is commonly credited with the authorship of *Hardyknute, a fragment of an antient Scots poem*,[29] which was first published in 1719 and reprinted throughout the century, soon becoming one of those texts that were recruited for the formation of post-Union literary Scottish identity in the 1760s.[30] With *Hardyknute*, Lady Wardlaw anticipated the interest that the reading public would take in Macpherson's pseudo-originals of Scots epic. According to Mel Kersey, "*Hardyknute* represents much more than a mere bibliographical curiosity, or simple 'fake'; it indicates the extent to which nationhood, in the broadest sense, thrives on myth-making and imagined sources." She notes that *Hardyknute* "re-imagines a chivalric, heroic Scottish past in order to influence the received image of Scotland's commitment to the Union."[31] It was issued jointly with the "Chevy-Chase" ballad in Aberdeen in 1754. Allan Ramsay, the pro-Union poet writing in a new-minted Scots, had included it in the *Evergreen* and the *Tea-Table Miscellany*, and Thomas Warton reprinted it in his miscellany, *The Union*. In 1781, John Pinkerton (1758–1826) invented a sequel to *Hardyknute*, and two years later an edition of *Hardyknute* was published that offers some insight into the strategies that readers applied to understand the poem as a whole, at the same time conceding its generic hybridity and its ruptured nature. The anonymous commentator states in the notes to the poem that it "appears to be of the epico-lyric kind, blending in some degree the characters of each of these species."[32] The *in medias res* opening is read in terms of rupture, for the "Poet filled with his subject bursts forth at

A
FRAGMENT.

BEING THE

Firſt CANTO of an Epick Poem ;

WITH

General REMARKS, and NOTES.

Animos in Martia Bella
Verſibus exacuit.   Hor.

LONDON :

Printed for R. DODSLEY, at *Tully's-Head* in *Pall-Mall.*

M.DCCXL.

Lady Elizabeth Wardlaw, *Harðyknute: A Fragment. Being the firſt Canto of an Epick Poem; with General Remarkʃ, and Noteʃ* (London: printed for R. Dodsley, 1740). Reproduced from a copy, and by permission, of the Beinecke Rare Books and Manuscript Library, Yale University.

once in the praises of his hero, without even informing us of his name."[33]

The edition of *Hardyknute* published by Dodsley in 1740 was accompanied by "General Remarks upon Hardyknute," in which the author singles out "a Grandeur, a Majesty of Sentiment" and "a true Sublime, which nothing can surpass."[34] The writer attests the poem's authenticity as an heroic production and notes: "Our Author had at least form'd to himself a more extensive Plan than that which we find executed."[35] Although he insists that it would be inappropriate to compare the author of *Hardyknute* with that of "the matchless Iliad," the comparison is implicitly made, inducing the writer of "General Remarks" to state that "our Author was undoubtedly blest with a large Portion of the fiery Spirit of Homer."[36]

Thomas Gray, in a letter to Horace Walpole, commends the poem's authenticity and remarks that "I have been often told that the poem called Hardicanute (which I always admired, and still admire) was the work of somebody that lived a few years ago. This I do not at all believe, though it has evidently been retouched in places by some modern hand."[37] The later version of *Hardyknute* no longer has an apologetic preface but confidently uses pseudo-ancient Scots diction throughout the forty-two metrically irregular eight-line stanzas. Stanza 1 may serve as an example:

> Stately stept he east the wa,
> And stately stept he west,
> Full seventy zeirs he now had sene,
> With skerfs sevin zeirs of rest.
> He livit quhen Britons breach of faith
> Wroucht Scotland meikle wae:
> And ay his sword tauld to their cost,
> He was their deadly fae.
>
> (1–8)

When Thomas Percy (1729–1811), the Bishop of Dromore, published his *Reliques of Ancient Poetry* (1765), he made available balladic texts such as *Hardyknute*. However, Percy introduces the following note, shedding further light on the poem's authenticity:

As this fine morsel of heroic poetry hath generally past for ancient, it is here thrown to the end of our earliest pieces; that such as doubt of its age, may the better compare it with other pieces of genuine antiquity.

> For after all, there is more than reason to suspect, that it owes most of its beauties (if not its whole existence) to the pen of a lady, within the present century. The following particulars may be depended on. Mrs. Wardlaw whose maiden name was Halket . . . pretended she had found this poem, written on shreds of paper employed for what is called the bottoms of clues. A suspicion arose that it was her own composition. Some able judges asserted it to be modern. The lady did in a manner acknowledge it to be so. Being desired to shew an additional stanza, as a proof of this, she produced the two last, beginning with '*There nae light*', &c. which were not in the copy that was first printed. . . . [However] the late William Thompson, the Scottish musician, who published the 'Orpheus Caledonius', 1735, 2 vols. 8vo. declared he had heard Fragments of it repeated in his infancy, before Mrs. Wardlaw's copy was heard of.[38]

Percy's note still retains an aspect of ambiguity, and he does not seem to be sure whether to classify it definitively as a fake. He concludes by using a defense that indicates that this fragment (or at least part of it) may be an original after all. Apart from *Hardyknute*, Percy included two further fragments, "The Ancient Fragment of the Marriage of Sir Gawaine" and "King Arthur's Death. A Fragment." The prefatory note to "The Ancient Fragment of the Marriage of Sir Gawaine" focuses on the nature of the fragmentary state of the poem: "The Second Poem in the third Series, intitled 'The Marriage of Sir Gawaine', having been offered to the Reader with large conjectural Supplements and Corrections, the old Fragment itself is here literally and exactly printed from the Editor's folio MS. With all its defects, inaccuracies, and errata."[39] The editor Percy uses the conventional apology for imperfection that is used throughout the eighteenth century by editors and authors (whether acknowledged or not) alike. Rather than making an attempt to "improve" the fragment, however, he is content to preserve it in its "defective" state as an authentic literary fragment.

Gray's "The Fatal Sisters" (1768), drafted in his commonplace book under the title of "The Song of the Weïrd Sisters, or Valkyries," reflects the appropriation of an Old Norse text by means of a poetic translation. In the process of the translation, Gray highlights specific concerns and ideas, and fragments the original text by rendering both its lexis and mythological ideology into English. As Gray's knowledge of Old Norse was insufficient to translate from the original, he translated the Latin translation that Arni Magnússon had provided. Roger Lonsdale suggests that Gray "may have tried to imitate the characteristic rhythms of the original Norse verse."[40] How selective Gray's process of translating was, is evidenced by his transcribing "the Latin texts in full, [whereas] he omitted much of the original Norse, and . . . reproduced errors which occur in the Latin."[41] In doing so, Gray created a new text, a text that the printer divided into stanzaic units, which Gray did not choose for the manuscript of his poem.

The fragmentariness of the context of the poem is counteracted by Gray's Preface, in which he explains both the setting and the myth, focusing on the Valkyries, "twelve gigantic figures resembling women: they were all employed about a loom; and as they wove, they sing the following dreadful Song; which when they had finished, they tore the web into twelve pieces, and (each taking a portion) galloped six to the north and as many to the south."[42] Gray uses a literal translation of the Latin and translates this poetically to include the drama of the weaving of the web. He avoids the direct balladic refrain—central to the original—"Let us weave, let us weave / The web of Darrad," which he introduces parenthetically as "Weave the crimson web of war" in "The Fatal Sisters."

ᑦᕒᕽ

In the mid-century, the fashion for writing fragments shifted from imitations of classical epic texts to texts that were contextualized within the framework of the revival of ancient (British) texts that had been stimulated by Addison's *Spectator* papers on primitive genius. In the *Spectator* papers 70, 71, and 85, Addison had provided ballad criticism that brought the genre to notice and insisted on its generic connection to the oral epic. John Bancks, in his definition of the ballad genre, also points to the generic relation:

A Sort of historical Compositions, rehearsing some memorable Action or Event in unpolished Numbers, which the People sung in a Manner no less rude and uncouth. What I have heard or read concerning the most remote Traces of Antiquity in every Nation, confirms me in this Opinion. The Rhythms of the Goths, and other Northern Nations, the Poetry of the antient Bards and Druids, that of the Americans in their first Discovery by the Spaniards that, in a Word, of Italy and Greece themselves in their primitive State, what was it but a Register of the remarkable Facts, Doctrines, and Institutions of the Heroes and great Men, which were transmitted from Generation to Generation, before the Use of Letters was invented?[43]

As an antiquarian and collector of medieval manuscripts, Thomas Percy
helped to foster the discourse of irregularity and fragmentariness that
had been introduced by imitations such as West's. In the Preface to *Five
Pieces of Runic Poetry* (1763), Percy considers the Runic productions he
translates as reflective of the character of the "SCALDS." He characterizes the "ancient inhabitants of the northern parts of Europe" as a
"hardy and unpolished race."[44] This "unpolished" character is reflected
in the spontaneous as well as "the rougher cast"[45] of their poetry. While
Percy insists on the exactness of his translations of Runic poetry, he
nevertheless notes his editorial method of appropriating this originally
Scaldic poetry to the compositional standards of the eighteenth century:

> Sometimes indeed, where a sentence was obscure, he hath ventured to
> drop it, and the asterisks which occur will denote such omissions. Some-
> times for the sake of perspicuity it was necessary to alter the arrange-
> ment of a period; and sometimes to throw in a few explanatory words:
> and even once or twice to substitute a more simple expression instead of
> the complex and enigmatic phrase of the original.[46]

He is aware that his own fragmentation of the text—with, to him, justi-
fiable editorially introduced elisions and omissions—does not contribute to establishing an eighteenth-century notion of "taste or classic
elegance," but that it serves "at least to unlock the treasures of native
genius."[47] Percy thus used the fragmentary to emphasize the "genius" of
these original Runic compositions.

Percy's *Five Pieces of Runic Poetry*—like Gray's translations of Old
Norse poetry—are appropriations. The indefinite "Pieces" are part of a
body of Runic poetry, a fragment of which is introduced in Percy's poetic renderings. The compositions that Percy reproduces are not introduced as discrete units, but—like the relics published by Charlotte
Brooke later in the century—represent an attempt at monumentalizing
a foreign literature, a process that was to find more prominent expression in Macpherson's *Fragments of Ancient Poetry*. Percy's "pieces" are in
fact broken off from their original context by the translator's poetic appropriation and demonstrate a strangeness that is clearly signaled to the
contemporary reader by means of the engraved Icelandic text on the
title page. The decontextualizing of these "pieces" further fragments
otherwise fragmentary poems, and through efforts such as Percy's and
Gray's, legitimized the mode in literature from the mid-1760s.

Through publications such as *Hardyknute* and Percy's *Reliques*, a taste
for the "Gothic" was being popularized that did not focus on imitating

FIVE PIECES

OF

RUNIC POETRY.

Tranflated from the

ISLANDIC LANGUAGE.

ᛒᛁᚱ ᛁᚠ ᚼᛁᛒᛁᛘ ᚤᛁᚼ ᚠ.
ᛋᚤᚼᛋ ᚤᚼᛁᚱᚠ ᛊᚤᚼᛁᛚ.
ᛊᚤᚠᛁᛏ ᚤᛁᛁᛘ ᛁᚠ ᛙᚤ.

* * * *Egill's Ode.*

ᚦᚱᛁᚤᚾᚤ ᛒᛁᛘᚱ ᛁᚠᛒᚱᛁᚠᛙ
ᚾᚱ ᛒᛁᚾᚤᚾᛁᚦᚾᚤ ᛊᛁᚾᛋᛁ.
ᛙᛁᚠᛘᛁᛘ ᛋᚤᛁᚠ ᛁᚠ ᛝᛁᛁ

————Populi, quos defpicit Arctos,
Felices errore fuo, quos ille timorum
Maximus haud urget leti metus : inde ruendi
In ferrum mens prona viris, animæque capaces
Mortis ; et ignavum redituræ parcere vitæ.

LUCAN.

LONDON:

Printed for R. and J. DODSLEY, in Pall-mall.

MD CC LXIII.

Thomas Percy, *Five Pieces of Runic Poetry. Translated from the Icelandic Language* (London: printed for R. and J. Dodsley, 1763). Reproduced from a copy, and by permission, of the Founders' Library, University of Wales, Lampeter.

the ancients but aimed to produce a cultural and national basis for post-Union Scottish identity. The Scottish were eager to celebrate what they considered as their "primitive" national literature, regarding it as an appropriate expression of the national character of the North as opposed to the *belles lettres* of the cultivated South. At last Scotland had prepared for an epic, which was published by James Macpherson (1736–96) as *Fragments of Ancient Poetry Collected in the Highlands of Scotland, and translated from the Galic or Erse Language* in 1760. This publication was followed by two further productions, *Fingal* (1761) and *Temora* (1763). Howard D. Weinbrot observes that:

> Ossian is the idealized treatment, or consequence, of the victory of the Moderns over the Ancients, of the expansion of literature in English beyond specifically English borders and concerns, and of the emerging definition of "British" that includes far more than Anglo-Saxon mythology, history, and literature.[48]

Macpherson's Ossianic works advertised themselves, and were read, as religious, cultural, and mythic relics. Fiona F. Stafford observes that the *Fragments* captured the "overwhelming sense of a world in the process of disintegration." She points out:

> The very form (or formlessness) of the poetry, though apparently reflecting the unrestrained passions of primitive man, could in fact be seen as a disintegration of orderly Augustan verse. For Macpherson and Blair, the *Fragments* were not even complete poems, but the broken remains of "a greater work": the dregs of a culture, rather than the essence. This very feeling gave the volume of 1760 an ephemeral quality, which disappeared in the more substantial "epics" that followed.[49]

Macpherson claimed to have discovered these pieces and declared that his function in publishing them was only that of a translator. His work was widely imitated, and in 1765 *The Battle of the Genii. A Fragment. In three cantos* was published, announcing itself as "Taken from an Erse manuscript, supposed to be written by Caithbut, the Grandfather of Cuchullin."[50] The "translator"—the author of *Homer Travestie* (1767), Thomas Bridges—in order to establish the poem's authenticity insists that "From the Plan of this POEM it is highly probable Our great Milton took the Hint of the Battle of the FALLEN ANGELS." By relating the fragment intertextually to *Paradise Lost*, the author conjures up a history of influence that did not originally exist but that is constructed to validate the poem. Even before that, a "Fragment of an Irish Poem. Taken from a literal prose translation" had been published.[51] Importantly, the writers of the "Ossianic" tradition insisted on the genuineness of the pieces,[52] redefining the meaning of translation and appropriating it as a (not so easily penetrable) veil to conceal the literary fake.

Of course, West had claimed genuineness as a key criterion for his canto, too; yet he still embedded his production in a framework of poetic ancestry, and relied on the merit of his imitation of Spenser's allegory and language. Furthermore, West's poem was a juvenile production, whilst Macpherson's epics were aimed at a different readership —that is, at those who might buy his texts on the basis of the (Scottish) national culture and heritage depicted.[53] That Macpherson's project was far more ambitious than West's may be seen by the reaction it provoked.[54] Soon, it culminated in a controversy as to the authenticity of the texts of Ossian, and critics such as Thomas Gray and, most prominently, Samuel Johnson involved themselves in denouncing the productions as literary forgeries. In August 1760, shortly after the publication of *Fragments of Ancient Poetry*, Gray wrote to a number of his friends, raising the issues of the genuineness and authenticity of the originals of Macpherson's translations. Writing to William Mason late in August, Gray relates that David Hume has provided proof as to the authenticity of the compositions that is "more satisfactory than any thing I have yet met with on that Subject."[55] According to Paul Baines:

> Johnson objected to what he saw as the lack of manuscript evidence, the self-deceit of witnesses to the oral tradition, and the poor literary quality of the poems. These views were expressed freely on the tour of Scotland which Johnson undertook with Boswell in the late summer of 1773, and given prominence in the *Journey to the Western Islands of Scotland*, published early in 1775.[56]

The debate after the publication of *Fragments of Ancient Poetry* must have been so heated and considered of national importance that Hugh Blair could be convinced to produce a preface (attesting the authenticity of the text) that was appended to each edition from 1763.[57] This dissertation, however, did not convince the skeptics who still wished "that the authenticity had been more largely stated. A man who knows Dr Blair's character will undoubtedly take his word—but the gross of mankind, considering how much it is the fashion to be skeptic in reading, will demand proofs, not assertions."[58] Since Macpherson insisted on the genuineness of the texts and was supported by a number of leading scholars, a committee was set up to "[i]nquire into the Nature and Authenticity of the Poems of Ossian."[59] In the event, a "committee of the Highland Society, after a long investigation of the whole subject, returned an open verdict."[60]

Unlike West or Croxall, Macpherson did not employ any obvious strategy to justify his publication of the fragments. He simply stated at the beginning of his Preface that "the public may depend on the following fragments as genuine remains of ancient Scottish poetry. . . . Tradition, in the country where they were written, refers them to an era of the most remote antiquity."[61] Indications of the pieces' antiquity, according to Macpherson, were that Ossian treats Christianity "with disdain," a fact that is understood in the sense that "Christianity was not yet established in the country."[62] Horace Walpole characterized Macpherson's productions by referring to the fragmentary implications of the transitions that Pindar used in his odes, indirectly emphasizing the link between the Pindaric mode and the fragmentary. Macpherson's *Fragments*, according to Walpole, were produced "before rules were invented to make poetry difficult and dull. The transitions are as sudden as those in Pindar, but not so libertine; for they start into new thoughts on the subject, without wandering from it."[63] Later on in the century, so-called "editors" no longer saw any need to validate the authenticity of the pieces they reproduced. Charlotte Brooke, for example, in the lengthy preface to her *Reliques of Irish Poetry* (1789), only apologizes for her inability to render the true meaning of Irish into English.[64] A more interesting case, however, is that of Chatterton.

Thomas Chatterton (1752–70), the precocious Bristol youth, who claimed to have discovered the writings of the medieval monk, Thomas Rowley, but in fact "invented" this author, like earlier writers producing fragmentary compositions, concocted a story to authenticate his forgeries and thereby sparked a debate on the authenticity of the poems that, like the Ossianic controversy, puzzled the most eminent antiquaries of the time. Apart from those fragmentary poems that create a context of loss, Chatterton in "An Excelente Balade of Charitie" (1770) displays a grounded knowledge of genre that relates the poem to the oral culture that is part of a medieval past that numerous writers using the mode of the fragmentary used to authenticate their works. The antiquated spelling of the poem, together with the generic mention of the ballad, deliberately removes the poem from a sense of familiarity in terms of eighteenth-century poetics and situates it in the creative realm of "the gode Prieste Thomas Rowley." Chatterton provided a glossary to "make the language intelligible," defending his decision to send the poem to the *Town and Country Magazine* with the statement that "the Sentiment, Description, and Versification, are highly deserving the attention of the literati." Chatterton did not reveal his identity even as supposed editor, but introduces the persona of "D.B." who merely publishes a transcription of the poem, "As wroten" by Rowley. The explanatory glossary and contextual information further underscore the constructed credentials of "D.B." as a scholarly editor who has rescued the poems of Rowley from perishing.

Although denominating his poem a "balade," the poem is structurally more complex than the simple ballad stanza. The thirteen isometrical stanzas consist of seven lines, the first six of which are iambic pentameters, the last an alexandrine. Chatterton's use of the rhyme royal establishes the connection with Chaucer that he lexically constructs by means of archaic words derived from historical glossaries. In its use of the concluding alexandrine, however, Chatterton denominates Spenser as his real source of inspiration. Even the tension between the rhyme and a form that resembles the Spenserian stanza (which did not exist in 1464 when "the gode Prieste Rowley" is said to have produced the ballad) seems contrived and meant to emphasize the mode of the fragmentary that Chatterton deploys. The emphasis, too, in the prefatory note on description and sentiment contextualizes the poem in terms of midcentury poetics rather than the unsentimental Christian rhetoric of Chaucer's poetry. Indeed, the poem is descriptive and, in stanza 2, offers an observant account of the weather:

> The sun was glemeing in the middle of daie,
> Deadde still the aire, and eke the welken blue,
> When from the sea arist in drear arraie
> A hepe of cloudes of sable sullen hue,
> The which full fast unto the woodlande drewe,
> Hiltring attenes the sunnis fetive face,
> And the blacke tempeste swollen and gatherd up apace.[65]
>
> (8–14)

Like Macpherson, Chatterton responds to the anxiety about British identity by inventing the persona of Thomas Rowley, who is one of the last voices from the past that speaks clearly, even in the fragmented mode that prevents Chatterton from reproducing a more comprehensive corpus of Rowley's works. Nick Groom terms the poet's attempt at fashioning a past of heroism and religious devotion "a gorgeous vision of England and Englishness measured through the fantastical archaism

of invented language."[66] Chatterton deploys the associations of the fragment to evoke new contexts. Reading his works as forgeries rather than
as expressions of his undoubted originality is to misunderstand their
value.[67]

What West's and Croxall's productions, Macpherson's "Ossian" fakes,
and Chatterton's "Rowley" poems have in common is that they use the
mode of the fragmentary. Both West and Croxall claim that the original
was more comprehensive, and that the piece reproduced by the supposed editor is only a fraction of the whole. In the case of *The Faerie
Queene*, its earliest editors and commentators stressed that the romance-
epic is fragmentary and that some of the parts originally written have
not survived. This aspect of incompleteness—as demonstrated in Chapter 3—makes the epic vulnerable to early eighteenth-century formal
criticism, which stressed linearity and unity. At the same time, it also offers the opportunity for poets to imagine possible cantos to fill the
(structural and semantic) "gaps" and to impose an artificial sense of
unity onto a "Gothic" composition. Croxall, much more convincingly
than West, invents a story to authenticate the text. He even adopts the
persona of Nestor Ironside, builds up a family genealogy, and completely veils his true identity in order to conceal his deceptive forgery.
Both West and Croxall understand their productions as belonging to a
genre of the fragment that, although alluding to a more comprehensive
whole into which it may be integrated, is nevertheless to be received as
a production of unity and coherence.

Macpherson's fragments, unlike West's or Croxall's faked cantos,
neither have a complete and comprehensive framework of referentiality,
nor can they genuinely claim specific poetic ancestry as did West's or
Croxall's. Macpherson intends his fragments to be read as incomplete
parts of a larger epic work and context. By identifying his fragments as
genuine, he leads others to believe that there must be an original epic
from which these parts derived. Unlike West, he does not derive the
part from the whole; rather, his poetic strategy works the other way
round, for he (or his readers) infer the whole from the fragments he
publishes. Chatterton's "Rowley" poetry invites the reader to discover
not only the meaning of the vision that has the Rowley poet at its center
but also to unravel the complicated spelling system and the "specialized
vocabulary of over 1,800 words,"[68] which need to be continuously
checked against the entries in the glossaries he provides. Like Macpherson, but in more elaborate ways, he is concerned with recovery and discovery.

Most poets discussed in this chapter concern themselves with re-working the epic, which at the beginning of the eighteenth century was still considered the most sublime form in the hierarchy of genres. Yet they find a particular mode to deal with the epic, for they use the medium of the literary fake to create a part of the epic, a fragment. Si-multaneously, they re-invent the epic and fashion it in line with the "Gothic" taste of the time. While West is one of the earliest prominent voices to articulate his admiration for Spenser, Macpherson produced what Scotland had never had, a national epic. Comprehending these compositions as mere imitations leads to a misrepresentation of habits of literary production in the mid-eighteenth century. Macpherson's *Fragments of Ancient Poetry* was innovative, since the text was answering a longing for Scottish identity and literary heritage that the people of Scotland had not yet discovered. It is in this unique context of cultural construction and nation-building that Macpherson used the genre of the fragment to remedy the perceived lack of a Scottish literary identity, thereby completing ideationally—like the hymnal ode—the quest for identity and wholeness.

The 1760s marked a turning point in terms of the acceptability of the fragmentary when Macpherson's productions, under the guise of being authentic fragments of original Gaelic materials, were published and le-gitimized by detailed commentaries. These fragments not only enjoyed great popularity within the British Isles, but their influence also spread all over Europe, with poets such as Goethe and Klopstock producing significant imitations in the fragment mode. Almost at the same time, a "rage for ruins" was stimulated by excavation projects in the Mediter-ranean and in Egypt, which culminated in artifacts and images of ruins being made available not only to members of the aristocracy but to the learned middle classes as well. The ruin as yet another cultural manifes-tation of the fragmentary further facilitated the acceptance of the frag-ment as a form that was widespread, having a long history that had its origins in classical antiquity.

5

Ruins, or, the Syntax
of the Fragmentary

The pilgrim oft
At dead of night, 'mid his oraison hears
Aghast the voice of time, disparting tow'rs,
Tumbling all precipitate down-dash'd,
Rattling around, loud thund'ring to the Moon.
—John Dyer, *The Ruins of Rome*

THE FRAGMENTARY IS A MODE OF ENDLESS POSSIBILITIES, INVITING EVER
new responses and appropriations in media ranging from the written
word to architecture. In Balachandra Rajan's words, the "unfinished"—
one name for the elusive fragmentary—represents "the most insistent
form of resistance to closure" and the prime example of literary "inde-
terminacy."[1] It is a mode that "invites completeness,"[2] involving the
reader creatively with the act of completing (incomplete) structure and
meaning. In that regard, Jennifer Snead notes that fragmentary sculp-
ture "evokes in its spectators an affective response similar to that of
reading."[3] In the previous chapters, the literary strategies of the fragmentary have been analyzed with reference to the "Pindaric mode," the
long-poem, and the invention of new texts, fakes, by means of the fragmentary. This chapter aims to consider an emanation of the fragmentary that had wider cultural significance and that would also have affected poets utilizing the notion of the unfinished. My account draws on
Anne Janowitz's pioneering work on ruins in the period, *England's
Ruins: Poetic Purpose and the National Landscape* (1990), while focusing on
the poetics of the ruinous. I shall briefly consider the "rage" for ruins in
the mid-century, as well as poetic examples of ruins such as John
Dyer's *Ruins of Rome* (1740), which not only considers the fragmentary
and ruinous as representing a monument of the past but also contextu-

108

alizes the "deliberate" ruin as a construct that can be comprehended in terms of the sublime. A consideration of George Keate's *Netley Abbey* (1769) will complement my discussion of Dyer's classical ruins and highlight the different ways in which these two poets deploy the ruinous. The chapter will conclude with a discussion of *An Elegy Written among the Ruins of an Abbey* (1765) by Edward Jerningham and the ways in which the poet engaged with the elegized past. Elegies point to the speaker's internalization of atmosphere rather than what Rothstein terms a "typical" speaker without individual identity. In that regard, in a poet's encounter with the ruinous, the ruin—in its fragmentary state—mirrors human frailty and becomes a *memento mori* of the futility of human life. Unlike the mid-century Pindaric ode, which frequently aimed to complete the incomplete and fallen identity of the poet, staging the poet's supplicating prayer to the deity to confer inspiration and wholeness, the ruin emphasizes and impresses upon the spectator's mind this very fragmentation, a fragmentariness that Young poetically invoked in *Night Thoughts*.

THE MATERIAL RUIN

Apart from the more traditional educational mode of traveling to Italy and France—the Grand Tour—the foundation of the Society of Dilettanti enabled men of fortune to travel to the continent, collect art, and employ artists to engrave their purchases. With the discoveries of Herculaneum (1739) and Pompeii (1748), a publishing industry had been started that reproduced not only the architecture and art of these cities but their ruins, too.[4] The immediate results of this new antiquarian fascination with the materialism of the past, especially ruins, were Robert Wood's *The Ruins of Palmyra* (1753) and *The Ruins of Balbec* (1757), Robert Sayer's *The Ruins of Athens* (1759), followed by Thomas Major's *The Ruins of Paestum* (1768), among many other beautifully and expensively engraved tomes. The destruction caused by the 1755 Lisbon earthquake also stimulated the production of engraved plates of the ruins of the city, with a collection of prints being published in 1756. When, in 1753, engraved plates of the ruins of Palmyra were published, Wood distinguished between two kinds of ruins: "We thought we could easily distinguish, at Palmyra, the ruins of two very different periods of antiquity, the decay of the oldest, which are meer rubbish, and incapable of measurement, looked like the gradual works of time; but the later seemed to bear the marks of violence."[5]

Although Wood does not explicitly deal with the fragment, his statement provides an insight into the poetics of the fragmentary; those buildings and monuments that have (naturally) disintegrated into ruins because of erosion and natural forces are not deliberate, they are gradual and do not reveal any human interference or intention culminating in their demolition. By contrast, those ruins that have been destroyed by man through violence possess marks of willful and deliberate destruction—being motivated by destructive intention—indicating an attempt to fragment and explode the apparent perfection (that is, power and authority) and architectural achievement of the enemy. Clearly, those ruins that have been affected by natural forces are less interesting to an age that connects violence with creativity and the sublime. Burke celebrates disorder in terms of the sublime, arguing that "apparent disorder augments . . . grandeur, for the appearance of care is highly contrary to our idea of magnificence."[6] The sheer number of constitutive, discrete, and disjointed elements of ruins represents "a richness and profusion of images, in which the mind is so dazzled as to make it impossible to attend to . . . [ideas of] exact coherence."[7] In addition, the "smoothness" of surfaces that characterizes Burke's notion of the beautiful disappears in the ruin in favor of "a broken and rugged surface,"[8] which is sublime. Those ruins whose disintegration was effected by means of violence become instances of sublimity in that they assert a cause and a notion of suffering that the personified building structure—now a ruin—had to undergo. In that regard, "deliberate" ruins not only "evoke an awareness of past accomplishment and present loss";[9] rather, they emphasize the validity of the cause they represented before their transformative creation. Architectural follies, which of course do not have the real association with the past that makes them sublime—by emulating the "marks of violence" mentioned by Wood— draw on the associations of a ruin that was deliberately created, not for the ruin's sake, but for the gratification of those who understood this destructive act as a means to assert and emblematize their authority.

Engraved images of ruins served a number of purposes in the eighteenth century: they provided material for architectural case studies and would occasionally reconstruct the ruin into a structure that was virtually complete. At times, ruins were printed in architectural manuals, historiographical works, or antiquarian "Beauties," demonstrating not so much their historicity as their style. By contrast, historical tableaux, heroic prints, or engravings reconstructing battle scenes could represent the ruins as disordered, incoherent, and scattered. Only with

Thomas Major, *The Ruins of Paestum. Otherwise Posidonia, in Magna Græcia*
(London: printed by James Dixwell, 1768). Reproduced from a copy, and
by permission, of the Founders' Library, University of Wales, Lampeter.

the antiquarian and proto-archaeological preoccupation to understand
the ruins of the past were attempts made at representing ruins more
exactly and accurately in their natural setting. Even this, however, was
frequently appropriated to various ideologies, serving or underscor-
ing a notion of British nationhood or the eighteenth-century endeavor
to imitate and reconstruct classical antiquity by erecting carefully
planned ruins in Britain. Depictions and visualizations of fragmentation were used in political terms, as in a century of party–political con-
flict, writers aimed to negotiate and dispel anxieties by establishing a
present that was superior to, and (at least) more stable than, the ruinous past.

An engraving of the then recently discovered ruins of Paestum sub-
stantiates my notion of the constructedness of fragmentariness. The
style of representation indicates the engraver's intention of showing not
the fragmented ruin, but an architecturally perfect and complete Palla-

dian building, such as a temple, which typically represents classical Roman architectural style.

These ruins are the legacy of a glorious past; whilst corruption has disappeared, the ruins, on the whole, are intact and display only superficial signs of destruction, decay, or fragmentation. They are deliberately, even artfully, damaged and are "decorated" with grasses and plants that, unlike the more English moss-covered ruins, appear artificial and reflect the representational and ideological intention of demonstrating the perfection of classical architecture even in its fragmentary state. This type of ruin can therefore serve as a model for neoclassical British architecture and draw on the associative links that Roman culture had with political ideals such as liberty. These ruins demonstrate that they have withstood time and human attempts at destroying not only works of classical architecture but also the culture they engender. They become symbols of power that are translated into British culture by means of reconstruction. Unlike Shelley's broken statue of Ozymandias, these ruins—because of their lack of individuality—can be reappropriated and recontextualized; they cannot be understood as the vain belief articulated in the pedestal inscription of Shelley's sonnet—that is, as futile and transient.[10]

The classical ruin—as represented in engravings and paintings—is frequently embedded within frameworks of myth, history, and the sublime, functioning as a monument of the past and cultural memory. The "domestic" ruin—that is, the British ruin—by contrast, is of course also a reminder of the past, but it can equally effectively be comprehended as a symbol of nationhood, as Anne Janowitz has demonstrated. In *England's Ruins*, she writes of a convergence of the ruin motif—as in Dyer's poems—with the author's intention of representing Britain. The ruin metonymically adopts a number of functions. According to Janowitz, the "ruin provides an historical provenance for the conception of the British nation as immemorially ancient, and through its naturalization subsumes cultural and class difference into a conflated representation of Britain as nature's inevitable product."[11] In eighteenth-century Britain, there were both neoclassical and British (mostly Gothic-style) ruins, and each of these referred to different contextual frameworks of fragmentariness; the "historical provenance" mentioned by Janowitz, in that regard, conveyed and echoed the age and (cultural) meaning of those ruins seen in Italy and Greece. One important feature of engraved English ruins was that ecclesiastical structures were used to mediate anxieties about faith that the authors of graveyard poetry stressed in their

Samuel and Nathaniel Buck, "The South View of Halton Castle in the County of Chester" (c. 1720). Reproduced from a copy in the author's possession.

productions of the 1750s and 1760s. The ruin, by definition, encompasses the dialectic of fragmentariness and wholeness, and especially in national terms can be a more effective metaphor of power than an impressive architectural structure captured in a state of perfection. The ruin implies the diachronic, embodying experience, whereas the perfect monument is static and undynamic.

British ruins were frequently engraved in historical surveys, especially when these ruins had served as demarcation points between two countries such as England and Wales. Samuel and Nathaniel Buck's plates, especially those included in *A Collection of Engravings of Castles, Abbeys and Towns in England and Wales* (1720–40), were reprinted throughout the century. The above engraving of a ruin near Chester demonstrates relative wholeness (through an indication of its original, complete design), while at the same time indicating fragmentariness and dissolution.

This dissolution is historically explained by Welsh efforts to invade Chester. The remnants of these ruins (as well as the memorialized visual representation of them—and the associated occasion for their creation—in print) are illustrative of the pride that the proprietors took in heralding their fortifications as effective deterrents, protecting not only Chester, but English culture as well. These ruins, therefore, despite their dilapidation, are still associated with the strength that would originally have withstood the enemies' attacks. The caption describes the castle as a monument that did honor to its owner; at the same time, the proprietor's patriotism is emphasized by means of the ruin that has withstood the enemy and is now—in its imperfection—a perfect embodiment of the spirit that defended English soil.

In her account of ruins, Janowitz traces an explicit shift in the thought of eighteenth-century writers and commentators from "culture to nature."[12] Consequently, the perfect building functions as a "temporal and spatial construct"[13] that inevitably finds a "life" as a ruin or fragment. In other words, the ruin images printed in historical works—although monuments of the past—gain relevance for the present in that they confirm the heroic character of Britons. Paradoxically, the very aspect of fragmentariness and partial destruction is understood to confirm the stability of the present. The imagined "life" of the ruin suggested by Janowitz has potency for poets who commemorate the achievement of the past, write in the *vanitas* tradition, or are engaging with the emerging topoi of graveyard poetry. The erection of follies and artificial ruins further provided stimuli that could then be integrated in the poetic mythmaking of the past or serve as the occasion for sentimental and melancholy contemplation.

By the mid-century, ruins were an integral part of the landscape and the booming discipline of landscape gardening. For William Shenstone (1714–63)—the Shropshire gentleman poet of "rural elegance" who defied clear-cut structures but preferred "to entangle his walks, and wind his waters" and "to plant a walk in undulating curves"[14]—ruins represented an essential element of what he terms "picture gardening," noting that they "may be neither new to us, nor majestic, nor beautiful, yet afford that pleasing melancholy which proceeds from a reflection on decayed magnificence."[15] He observes in his "Unconnected Thoughts on Gardening" that:

> Ruinated structures appear to derive their power of pleasing, from the irregularity of surface; which is VARIETY; and the latitude they afford the imagination, to conceive an enlargement of their dimensions, or to recollect any events or circumstances appertaining to their pristine grandeur, so far as concerns grandeur and solemnity. The breaks in them should be as bold and abrupt as possible.[16]

Shenstone refers to two very different aspects of ruins. On the one hand, ruins are symbols of the past, reminiscent of past grandeur and sublimity. These, according to the poet, inspire awe and "solemnity."

On the other hand, the aesthetic ideal of variety is embodied in "bold and abrupt" "breaks," and integrates very well in a landscape that works on the basis of balance as well as contrasts. For Shenstone, the ruin becomes an essential feature of a landscaped garden, a feature that he introduced at his own *ferme ornée*, the Leasowes. Shenstone thereby followed the Japanese idea of *sharawadgi*, first popularized by Sir William Temple in "Upon the Gardens of Epicurus" (1685). Temple favored the Pindaric manner of gardening, noting that "there may be other forms [of gardens] wholly irregular that may . . . have more beauty than any of the [regular] others; but they must owe it to some extraordinary dispositions of nature in the seat, or some great race of fancy or judgment in the contrivance, which may reduce many disagreeing parts into some figure." This notion of *sharawadgi*—the "phenomenon of beauty occurring in the absence of discernible order and recurrent design"—was the ideal that Shenstone wanted to realize at the Leasowes.[17]

Shenstone, the man of letters, friend of Thomas Percy and Thomson, led a life that was devoted to improving his ornamental farm. A prolific poet, he used a large variety of poetic forms ranging from the comic Spenserian long-poem *The School-Mistress* and writings on gardening to an overt engagement—in the form of the long-poem—with the ruinous in *The Ruin'd Abbey*. Shenstone interpreted the ruinous as an organic state that could be emulated and imitated in (literary and horticultural) art. The tension between man-made structure and the control that man imposes on nature, and the natural forces that break the formerly splendid ruins, is voiced too by Shenstone when he notes that "the works of a person that builds, begin immediately to decay; while those of him who plants begin directly to improve."[18] Therefore, Shenstone argues, it is important to interfere with the natural order as gently as possible and to "improve" the perfect structure of nature by adding variety—that is, the fragmentary and the Pindaric in the ideal form of the ruin. He highlights that *natura naturans* needs the emulating assistance of man, in that a designed ruin is expected to be "as bold and abrupt as possible"—that is, subscribing to criteria that man has dictated.

Shenstone's comments on ruins can be understood in terms of nationhood as well. He uses "new" ruins to represent the past, but at the same time constructs the ruins so that he can inscribe them with a past of his own making. Janowitz's movement from culture to nature is thereby subtly and skillfully inverted. The ruin is thus transformed into a symbol of cultural sophistication and of the elite's fashioning of a past of their own that declares them as part of a tradition that, despite its ruinous emblematism, has survived the supposed ravages of time. It is in illustrations of follies and constructed ruins that modern critics such as Elizabeth Wanning Harries have discovered an underlying attempt at a "union of art and nature."[19] The "rage of ruins," in her view, reflected the "commodification of taste,"[20] a taste that was widely adopted into the cultural repertoire of landscape gardening. By contrast, Thomas McFarland, considering the ruin in a temporal context, states that the "present was a ruin of the past's possibilities."[21] In that respect, it no longer matters whether the ruins represented in works such as gardening manuals are authentic or not—"What matters is its [the ruin's] visual function."[22] The apparent eighteenth-century decontextualization and deracination of ruins (by means of illustration, reconstruction, or changing taste favoring architectural follies) from a framework of progress and decay take place in a vacuum of artistic stability. Nevertheless, "the artificial ruin . . . is a mock monument that ironizes its own pseudofunction as monument."[23] Ruins functioned as "mediators" between past and present. According to Harries, the "imagination of ruin helped people . . . to free themselves from the structures of the past, or at least to see them as temporary and mutable."[24]

LITERARY RUINS

The theme of ruins is by no means an exclusive eighteenth-century one. Edmund Spenser was fascinated by the theme of ruins. Building on the success of the first three books of *The Faerie Queene* and receiving inspiration from Joachim Du Bellay's (c. 1525–60) "ruin" sequence, *Les Antiquitez de Rome* (1558), Spenser translated a sequence of poems, which contained *The Ruines of Time* in 1591.[25] Du Bellay's *Les Antiquitez de Rome* pronounced the poet's ambivalence toward the ruin of the city and the possibility of renewal and restoration (both of Rome's architecture and its classical ideals). In Spenser's sequence, Ruin—in an allegorical garb—is the speaking persona through which the poet introduces and voices his reflections on the ruinous character of time: one moment man-made artifacts may be perfectly sound, whilst in the next they collapse under the destructive weight of time. Time, in that sense, is only too intent to assist ruin and thus to turn perfection, represented variously by golden achievement, into fragmented elements of loss, devastation, and decline. So, although the "Image, all of massie gold" inspired reverence and adoration, its physical base, "on which this Image staid, / Was (O great pitie) built of brickle clay," was not able to sustain the statue's weight and consequently collapsed. Ruin, as speaking personification, however, does not proudly demonstrate and declaim her triumph over human (or, more generally, terrestrial) existence, but laments the inevitability of everything that the personification represents:

> But whie (vnhappie wight) doo I thus crie,
> And grieue that my remembrance quite is raced
> Out of the knowledge of posteritie,
> And all my antique monuments defaced?
> Sith I doo dailie see things highest placed,
> So soone as fates their vitall thred haue shorne,
> Forgotten quite as they were neuer borne.
>
> (176–82)

The personification can completely identify with both the gradual or sudden demolition of monuments that had been conceptualized by their makers as eternal manifestations of the glory of mankind. It becomes clear that Ruin aspires to divine permanence, to an elevation beyond terrestrial temporality and transience, as well as to be part of a metaphorical edifice that will survive all change. In reality, however, Ruin stands for the "rustie darkness" of oblivion, loss of memory, and the awareness of survival in the cultural memory of humankind as an unlikely prospect.

In the eighteenth century the ruin became an integral component of graveyard poetry, a body of poetry comprising *memento mori* productions in the *vanitas* tradition that reflected political and religious instabilities and found such diverse expressions as Gray's "Elegy Wrote in a Country Churchyard" and Young's *Night Thoughts*. Graveyard poems, however, were written as early as the 1720s, disseminated in the form of funeral elegies, contemplative pieces on death, and long meditations such as Robert Blair's *The Grave*. The ruins that figured in the descriptive poetry of the period became a stock motif in elegies that were printed in the wake of Gray's "Elegy."

A personified Ruin featured in David Mallet's *The Excursion* (1728), a discursive poem that uses the descriptive impulses of Scottish poetry and that Johnson defined in terms of "striking" images and "elegant" "paragraphs," representing "a desultory and capricious view of such scenes of Nature as his [Mallet's] fancy led him, or his knowledge enabled him, to describe."[26] In Mallet's poem, Ruin regrets neither the disintegration of the past, nor the decay of human effort and achievement. Ruin is introduced into a Gothic landscape and described as sitting on a "reverend pile," "brooding o'er sightless skulls, and crumbling bones." In Mallet's long-poem, Ruin has particularly graphic and ecphrastic authority and is one of the personification deities whom Mallet's speaker meets on his "excursive" quest.

A designatedly British ruin features in a poem that Mallet's acquaintance, John Dyer, completed in 1726. There are two main versions of "Grongar Hill," the poem for which Dyer (1699–58), a Welsh poet, painter, and parson, is primarily remembered today. His poem is associated with the first version of Thomson's *Winter* and the making of Mallet's *Excursion*, and Dyer was indeed on friendly terms with these poets while he was a member of Aaron Hill's literary coterie in the 1720s.[27] In the Pindaric version of the poem (printed for the first time in Richard Savage's *Miscellaneous Poems and Translations* of 1726), the speaker feels overwhelmed at the sight of the ruins of the castles that he can see when ascending his favorite mountain.[28] He introduces the castle ruin and then adds a digression on the vanity of human power, acknowledging at the same time the all-invasive and pervasive force of nature. While William Gilpin censured the poem's lack of picturesque qualities that would have "melt[ed] a variety of objects into one rich whole,"[29] Dyer's intention is to introduce the ruin as a concrete phenomenon of the landscape and then derive a moralizing digression from it. In the first instance, the depiction of the ruin follows a dramatic description of the "bord'ring Flood" of the river and the "sullen Wood," as well as a "steep Hill [that] starts horrid, wild, and, high." The earliest version of "Grongar Hill" ends the description of the sublime landscape by introducing the ancient towers seen in the distance:

> Towers, ancient as the Mountain, crown its Brow,
> Aweful in Ruin, to the Plains below.
> Thick round the ragged Walls pale Ivy creeps,
> While circling Arms the nodding Fabrick keeps;
> While both combine to check th'insulting Wind,
> As Friends, in Danger, mutual Comfort find.[30]
>
> (73–78)

A later version of "Grongar Hill" highlighted the agency of the ruins:

> And ancient towers crown his brow,
> That cast an aweful look below;

Whose ragged walls the ivy creeps,
And with her arms from falling keeps;
So both a safety from the wind
On mutual dependence find.

(71–76)

Dyer aestheticizes the ruin and elevates it to the status of a natural phenomenon of sublimity, as Shelley would do more elaborately with Mont
Blanc. The poet's aestheticized ruin is described as having developed
rather than decayed from a perfect architectural structure; generically,
Dyer sees the fragmentary as a state that is not inferior to the perfect
original building but that represents McGann's evolutionary idea of the
textual condition. The ruin, therefore, is the temporary result of a transformative process that has changed its mode of containment and translated it into a construct of the fragmentary sublime.

So, while Dyer admits that the ruins he perceives are in decay, he
yet emphasizes that these ruinous remnants of buildings have entered
an organic unity with the ivy that supports the structure of the ruin
and keeps it from collapse. The decay of the ruin is thereby superfi-
cially halted; however, while the ivy may provide the support needed
for the moment, it nevertheless will ultimately take over and assist the
"insulting wind" in demolishing the ruin completely. It will destroy the
unfinished and processual structure and transform it into rubbish,
thereby negating its "identity" as a ruin. Also, Dyer ignores the rules of
painterly perspective and foregrounds the ruin; although the ruin in
the background should have been described in colors less striking and
prominent, he describes it in very prominent and eye-catching terms
that move the ruin to a more central place than it in fact occupies.

In the later octosyllabic version of "Grongar Hill" (which was printed in David Lewis's *Miscellany* [July 1726] and in which Dyer transformed the Pindaric character of the poem into a regular division into
trochaic tetrameters), nature—represented by the toad, the fox, and the
"pois'nous adder"—has invaded the ruin.[31] The "hoary moulder'd walls"
that have "survived" are now being changed and, "[c]onceal'd in ruins,
moss, and weeds," will ultimately disappear in and be absorbed by the
landscape. In that sense, Dyer, as has been pointed out by Stuart Piggot, has already anticipated the view assumed in the mid-century—that
is, that "ruins were . . . very much a part of the landscape, to be seen
and appreciated from more than one viewpoint."[32] The traditional seventeenth-century reproach that "Gothic architecture was a non-classical

muddle, and as such unworthy of the Man of Taste" and that it was a "style barbare"[33] was now being given up in favor of considering Gothic ruins as inherent parts of the English landscape.

In his long-poem, *The Ruins of Rome*, Dyer praises the kind of ruin that has not been created by time but by human destructive force. He started the poem in the mid-1720s while he studied under the guidance of the eminent painter, Jonathan Richardson, and undertook a journey to Italy to improve his painting skills there.[34] He considers the ruins of Rome:

> Ev'n yet majestical; the solemn scene
> Elates the soul, while now the rising sun
> Flames on the ruins in the purer air
> Tow'ring aloft, upon the glitt'ring plain,
> Like broken rocks, a vast circumference;
> Rent palaces, crush'd columns, rifted moles,
> Fanes roll'd on fanes, and tombs on buried tombs.[35]

He describes the ruins in terms of "broken rocks," mentioning the "crush'd columns" and "rifted moles." The adjectives that Dyer uses indicate that an enormous destructive force was applied to the formerly magnificent buildings of Rome to create these "majestical" ruins. In the same vein, *The Beauties of British Antiquity* reproduces an essay on Stonehenge, terming it a "venerable pile."[36] Writing of ruinous and fragmented monastic buildings, the author notes that the "solemn ruins of the abbey strike the mind with reverential awe and serious reflection,"[37] a response that is echoed variously by heroines of Gothic novels.

George Keate (1730–97), a minor poet and significant mid-century man of letters, not only produced the Miltonic poem, *The Alps: A Poem* (1763), but also published *Netley Abbey. An Elegy*, which adopts an approach to the ruin that is markedly different from Dyer's.[38] Keate imitated the *Ruins of Rome* in his ambitious blank verse poem, *Ancient and Modern Rome* (1760), the title of which was reminiscent of the first part of Thomson's *Liberty*. In *Netley Abbey*, he celebrates the ruin of the abbey, which is situated near Southampton, in terms of (moral) integrity and active virtue. Kathryn Gilbert Dapp notes that the production is expressive of "a romantic attitude compounded of reverence, exultation, pensive melancholy, and platitudinous moralizing" but observes that Keate "paid tribute to 'RELIGION' as a great protectress of the arts."[39]

NETLEY ABBEY.

AN ELEGY.

BY

GEORGE KEATE, Efq;

The SECOND EDITION, corrected and enlarged.

Horrendum Sylvis et Relligione parentum.

VIRGIL.

LONDON,

Printed for J. DODSLEY, in *Pall-Mall*, MDCCLXIX.

Title-page of George Keate's *Netley Abbey. An Elegy* (London: printed for J. Dodsley, 1769). Reproduced from a copy in the author's possession.

The poem was printed in 1764, but significantly revised for its second edition of 1769. Keate states in his introductory essay that he "collected some scattered Particulars together, separating as much as possible the fabulous and historical Traditions concerning its Fates, since the general Dissolution of Religious Houses in this Kingdom."[40] The poem undertakes the defense of the abbey—this "venerable Piece of Antiquity"—against the many "Depredations"[41] it has encountered in the course of its long history. Keate provides an historical account of the building in the preface but offers little in the poem to enable the reader to gain a sense of the historical anatomy of Netley Abbey. While Dyer "assembles the great ruined buildings of Rome into a grand and processional arrangement, rather than into a just representation of the early eighteenth-century disorder of the city,"[42] Keate explores the ruin's life, as well as its apparent contest for a continued existence. He does not follow an agenda of Whig progress (as does Dyer) but produces an elegy (and eventual epitaph) on the abbey in which he glorifies the ruinous and fragmentary character of the building as an expression of the life and strength not only of the physical abbey, but of its associations with religion as well. He, therefore, concludes his introductory essay by stating that:

> the ingenious author modestly desires it may be understood, that neither the one nor the other [his two versions of Netley Abbey] were made in consequence of any supposed merit of its own, but merely to preserve the memory of an ancient ruin, which has alternately suffered from the weather, and the ill taste of its owners, to such a degree, that they who seek it a few years hence, may find it only in this description.[43]

The ruins of the abbey are presented animistically, dominating the landscape in "melancholy Greatness." The speaker deplores the changes that have affected the abbey's "proud Majesty" but insists that it has transformed into a ruin to defend itself against "Some rude Dismantler" who, as Keate noted in the prefatory essay, was killed by tumbling fragments of the edifice:

> The menac'd Arches frown'd,
> The conscious Walls in sudden Conflict join'd,
> Crush'd the pale Wretch in one promiscuous Wound,
> And left this Monument of Wrath behind.

Keate linguistically confers agency on the walls of the abbey, observing that "Now sunk, deserted, and with Weeds o'ergrown, / Yon prostrate Walls their harder Fate bewail." While external forces are affecting the building structure, the abbey asserts its agency still by contesting man's commercial and sacrilegious, rather than spiritual, authority over it. The "shatter'd Pile" appears to have come to life once the organized ecclesiastical structures that guided religious practice at the abbey disappeared. The repeated introduction of fate links the ruin with humanity in that the life of the building is affected by a decreed series of events that will culminate in the complete disintegration of the structure. This, however, the poet does not depict, except for instances where anthropomorphized elements of the ruin can no longer withstand the external pressures of disintegration. In that regard, "the Gothic Pillars [sic] slender Form" "Deserts its Post, and reeling to the Storm, / With sullen Crash resigns its Charge to Fate." Parts of the abbey are dying, but in *Netley Abbey* the ruin stands for the persistent belief in life rather than the finality of complete disintegration. This assertion of life against all odds, and the visually ruinous state of the abbey fascinate and attract those who view and contemplate the ruin; the "proud cumb'rous Mass" thereby recruits the human interest that was lost when the ecclesiastical foundation was abandoned and yet manages to resist the closure that its disappearance would entail.

In *The Cure of Saul. A Sacred Ode* (1763), John Brown introduces Ruin as a force that, called upon by God, leaves its subterranean prison in order to vindicate God's power and—nemesis-like—remind man of his fallibility and sins. It is "th' avenging God" who sends the personification among humanity:

> "*Ruin*, lift thy baleful Head;
> "Rouze the guilty World from Sleep:
> "Lead up thy Billows from their cavern'd Bed,
> "And burst the Rocks that chain thee in the Deep. —[44]

Ruin serves as a reminder of God's potential wrath and the consequences of a life of Hate and Envy, Rage and Lust, which will inevitably culminate in an existence in the hellish subterranean realm of Ruin.[45] Both Keate and Brown deploy Ruin in pseudoreligious contexts; while the former understands it as a force that has the ability to protect religious spirituality through its spectacular quality, the latter presents the personification in terms of a power that, if once let loose, will reestablish God's authority on earth.

THE RUIN AS A LOCUS

FOR CONTEMPLATION

In *The Ruin'd Abbey* (1764), Shenstone creates an analogy between the past, its corrupted splendor, ultimate decline, and the ruined abbey, which is the material remnant of cultural memory. It is in this context of symbolizing memory that the ruin is frequently encountered in mid- and late eighteenth-century poetry. Thomas Warton in *The Pleasures of Melancholy* (1747), in that regard, draws on his memories, which are enhanced by the presence and stimulating qualities of the ruin. His speaker, therefore, appeals to Melancholy to enable him to contemplate in solitude his past and his memories:

> Beneath yon ruin'd abbey's moss-grown piles,
> Oft let me sit, at twilight hour of eve,
> Where thro' some Western window the pale Moon
> Pours her long-levell'd rule of streaming light;
> While sullen sacred silence reigns around,
> Save the lone screech-owl's note, who builds his bow'r
> Amid the mould'ring caverns dark and damp,
> Of the calm breeze, that rustles in the leaves
> Of flaunting ivy, that with mantle green
> Invests some wasted tow'r.[46]
>
> (28–37)

The environment of the ruin provides a stimulus to contemplation and, in the descriptive-allegoric poetry of the mid-century, is often designated the haunt of Melancholy or Terror. Above all, the ruin represents forcefully the fragmentariness of human existence, but is also hope-inspiring in that, in Warton's poem, it is understood as a sacred place where the speaker can contemplate and, as in mid-century odes, invoke the deity for inspiration.

Edward Jerningham (1737–1812), Norwich poet and playwright, friend of Horace Walpole, and imitator of Gray and Mason, in *An Elegy Written among the Ruins of an Abbey* (1765) interprets the ruin as an emblem of superstition and haunt of those who were attracted to the powers of darkness rather than Christian faith. "Veil'd Superstition" inhabited the abbey and drew "Bad Albion's sons" from "the splendid Court":

> Alas! obsequious to her stern Command,
> A sullen-pensive Brotherhood they came,
> Refus'd to trace the Paths by Nature plan'd,
> And raz'd from Glory's Page their ancient Name.
>   (17–20)

With a glance at Thomson's *The Castle of Indolence*, Jerningham transforms the abbey from a place of spirituality into one of indolence and sloth. The reign of Superstition on her "tinsel'd Throne" is short, as Truth "[w]ith Hand unerring overthrew" the illusory authority of superstitious faith. The result is the demolition of the temples of superstition. The abbey is thereby transformed into a ruin that is inhabited by the fallen goddess:

> On yon Dust-level'd Spire the crafty Maid,
> With Indignation brooding in her Breast
> Sits gloomily—Her Vot'ries all are fled,
> Her Lamps extinguish'd, and her Rites suppress'd:
>   (29–32)

She surrounds herself with the insignia of her former power, such as the "blotted scroll" that "Contains the Maxims of her slighted Creed" and "a mould'ring Shrine" at her feet. No longer does she preside over the pile, but Ruin has invaded the abbey and "hovers round the desert Scene." The outside world of religion, however, is protected from the corrupting influence of the "shatter'd Pile" by "many a sordid Briar." Once Ruin, with the assistance of Truth, has usurped Superstition's power, the abbey becomes a monument of a time without Christian faith and enlightenment. Triumphing over the culture of superstition, the ruin is appropriated by Jerningham as a symbol of enlightenment, securely contained by the "Briars" but nevertheless present in the cultural consciousness to inspire reflection on true faith.

Although the ruin as a cultural metaphor—in its various emanations in the eighteenth century—did not invent the discourse and strategies of fragmentation outlined in the earlier chapters, it certainly provided an additional popularizing element in the legitimization process of the fragmentary and its subsequent introduction to a variety of disciplines.

Its discourse was culturally pervasive and negotiated in unique ways the traditional dichotomy of *natura naturata* and *natura naturans*. Above all, the ruin deployed the mode of the fragmentary not only structurally, but symbolically and psychologically as well, ultimately serving as a metaphor for Romantic memory.

6

Smith, Wordsworth, and the Fragments of Memory

> Chaotic pile of barren stone,
> That Nature's hurrying hand has thrown,
>   Half-finish'd, from the troubled waves;
> On whose rude brow the rifted tower
> Has frown'd, thro' many a stormy hour,
>   On this drear site of temper-beaten graves.
>
> — From Charlotte Smith, "A Descriptive Ode,
> Supposed to have been written under the ruins
> of Rufus's Castle, among the remains of the
> ancient Church on the Isle of Portland"

THIS CHAPTER FOCUSES ON TWO MAJOR ROMANTIC POEMS THAT — UN-like such productions as Coleridge's *Christabel*—have largely not been explored by critics of the Romantic fragment poem. Rather than reading them primarily in terms of their Romantic concerns, I shall explore the ways in which the poems use the various techniques of the eighteenth-century mode of the fragmentary. Poems such as Charlotte Smith's *Beachy Head* and Wordsworth's "Lines composed a few miles above Tintern Abbey, on revisiting the Banks of the Wye, during a Tour, July 13, 1798" have become central to our understanding of Romantic poetics and ideology, and a contextualization of these texts not only reinforces the awareness that both Smith and Wordsworth (and, more generally, all Romantics) emerged out of an eighteenth-century writing culture but that they also prominently used forms and modes that were popularized before the publication of the Romantic manifesto, *Lyrical Ballads* (1798).[1]

Charlotte Smith (1749–1806) was a widely read poet at the end of the eighteenth century and one of the foremost sonneteers of the period.[2] Her reputation as a writer was established through the publication of *Elegiac Sonnets* (1784, but republished in many subsequent, expanded editions) and a number of novels, of which *Emmeline* (1788) and *The Old Manor House* (1793) are probably the best known. She also produced a long-poem, *Beachy Head*, which was published posthumously in a collection entitled *Beachy Head, Fables, and Other Poems* (1807). From the moment of its first publication, the poem was considered formally problematic in that the editor of the posthumous collection felt the need to mention Smith's failing health, as if implicitly offering a defense of the poem's fragmentary form, for:

> most of the Poems included in this volume were composed during the few and short intervals of ease which her [Smith's] infirmities permitted her to enjoy; yet they bear the most unquestionable evidence of the same undiminished genius, spirit, and imagination, which so imminently distinguished her former productions.[3]

The editor's insistence on the author's "infirmities"—her failing strength and suffering—is here juxtaposed with Smith's "undiminished genius, spirit, and imagination." The reader anticipates the poem to have been written at a moment of crisis and that it cannot possibly—and this is reinforced through the Advertisement—be as "perfect" as Smith's previous work. Smith's nineteenth-century editor is quick to acknowledge the fragmentary character of *Beachy Head*: "The Poem entitled BEACHY HEAD is not completed according to the original design. That the increasing debility of its author has been the cause of its being left in an imperfect state, will it is hoped be a sufficient apology."[4]

The editor's apology focuses on Smith's illness, which, according to the Advertisement, prevented the completion of the work in accordance with the "original design." He does not provide any indication of what this "original design" might have entailed, nor does he consider the possibility that Smith might have intended the fragmentary character for which he sees the need to apologize. By prefixing an explanatory Advertisement to the work, the editor draws on a technique that throughout this study has been shown to be variously used as a defense of, or apology for, both the fragment form and the mode of the fragmentary. Smith's editor uses his prefatory statement to authenticate Smith's poetry but also to legitimize—at least to a certain extent—the form of *Beachy Head*.

The idea of the fragment is not only structural, but, from the start of the poem, it is topical. Rather than understanding *Beachy Head* as a formal fragment that is characterized by a sense of incompletion and the unfinished only, Smith's ruminating speaker counteracts any sense of stasis and stability by wandering across and surveying the landscape, not seeing it as a whole but as a disjunctive ensemble of fragments that reflect the speaker's incoherent state of mind. John M. Anderson, describing the poem's structural fragmentariness, observes that it is "a majestic fragment . . . left enticingly unfinished. But the introduction of this stranger [the visionary poet], dwelling by choice among the ruins, suggests that the fragmentary form of this poem is not entirely an accident—that Smith was attracted to the idea of constructing a ruin, a fragment expressively."[5] In fact, Smith's poem fits McFarland's "diasparactive triad" introduced at the beginning of this study.

The poem describes the creation of Beachy Head—through Nature—in terms of sublime forces. These forces separate the "stupendous summit, rock sublime" from the mainland of France. Smith adds an informative note that functions as a digressive distraction, fragmenting further the linear sequence of the poem's progress: "Alluding to an idea that this Island was once joined to the continent of Europe, and torn from it by some convulsion of Nature":

> Fancy should go forth,
> And represent the strange and awful hour
> Of vast concussion; when the Omnipotent
> Stretch'd forth his arm, and rent the solid hills,
> Bidding the impetuous main flood rush between
> The rifted shores, and from the continent
> Eternally divided this green isle.
>
> (4–10)

Smith represents the making of *Beachy Head* by means of imaginative recall in which Fancy accesses the memory of Nature (and Smith's imagination, of course) to turn a gradual process of drift into a sudden event and a moment in time that, through its abruptness, initiates an immediacy that articulates itself through fragmented (reflective, digressive, and observing) voices. The poet tries to complete a comprehensive vision of the landscape in which the shortcomings of both human sight and optical perspective are supplemented by historical digression, natural-scientific observation and reflection, and an emotional reworking of past pleasure and sublime experience.

The final part of the poem makes use of the word "fragment" twice and connects it with the existence of two outcasts of society. The very choice of outcasts, hermits who have willfully decided to leave the society and corruption of man, is illustrative of the poet's intention of showing the fragmentariness of the microcosm of Beachy Head.[6] Despite his desire to separate and isolate himself from human company, the first hermit (a poet) appears to exist in a limbo in which he cannot (yet) enter the sphere of complete solitude and happiness; rather, he has to find a way and mode of expressing the fragmentedness of his existence and his unique way of life by means of songs that reveal his story.

The hermit's life epitomizes the ruinated and disjunctive state of man. He has chosen his abode in a "castellated mansion," which, in former times, stood in the landscape as a symbol of power and stability. The poet-narrator's depiction sounds anecdotal as it is introduced by "once":

> In such a castellated mansion once
> A stranger chose his home; and where hard by
> In rude disorder fallen, and hid with brushwood
> Lay fragments gray of towers and buttresses,
> Among the ruins, often he would muse —
>
> (506–10)

The stability of the fortress has disappeared, and a change toward permanent flux, restlessness, and erratic wandering in search of a surrogate happiness has taken place. Smith reveals that the hermit's "senses [are] injur'd," but that he is finding solace and comfort "[a]mong the ruins, [where] often he would muse." Smith is aware of her inability to convey the meaning of the hermit's fragmented existence. For this reason, she inserts a lyric piece in which he expresses his longing to bring back the past and revive those moments when "once I walk'd with you" and "hear[d] your voice upon the gale." He implicitly addresses a memory of completeness, which, however, remains fragmented, unfulfilled, and unreciprocated. The generic hybridity of interspersing the narrative part of the hermit's wanderings with highly subjective lyrical pieces echoes his endeavor to overcome the incoherence of his life by trying to establish a personal and coherent "lyrical" voice. At the same time, he absorbs and identifies with the fragmented character of the ruin. Lyrical performativity, therefore, like the oral epic, serves to realize a comprehensive vision coherently by means of drama, emotion, and recitation, whereas scripturality can only in a limited way resemble the fullness of the hermit's longings and his re-evocation of past happiness.

Although, physically, the poet still lives within a human context, he has retired to a world created by his imagination in which he can re-evoke and re-experience the bliss he used to experience before: "And in his wanderings, [he] rear'd to sooth his soul / Ideal bowers of pleasure." External life becomes unimportant to him, as he enters a spiritual nature-adoring existence that simple people such as woodmen cannot properly interpret; he becomes an instance of the "other," and his wandering is compared to the haunting of a ghost:

> And then in silence, gliding like a ghost
> He vanish'd! Lost among the deepening gloom. —
> But near one ancient tree, whose wreathed roots
> Form'd a rude couch, love-songs and scatter'd rhymes,
> Unfinish'd sentences, or half-erased,
> And rhapsodies like this, were sometimes found.
>
> (571–76)

The "scatter'd rhymes" and "[u]nfinish'd sentences," "half-erased," symbolize the dissociation of his human existence; the meaningfulness of his life does not depend on his participating in social intercourse but consists in his absorption of nature. He has lost any clear direction according to which he may structure his life, and the adjective "half-erased" refers not only to the sentences of his songs, but also to the meaning of his being within a defined framework of social participation. Without the love that he praises and recollects in his songs, he has no purpose and meaning any more: he is merely a "fragment" — a broken piece — of his former self.

Smith's second hermit (whom she identifies in a note as a certain "Parson Darby") lives "Just beneath the rock / Where Beachy overpeers the channel wave, / Within a cavern mined with wintry tides." The "hermit of the rocks" has sought a home in a natural environment that to other people would be uninviting, cold, and frightening. It is an environment that is destructive, as the forces of the water invade the land and deprive human beings of their lives. He "appear'd to suffer life / Rather than live" and consider it his duty to bury those unfortunate men that found their untimely end in the waves of Beachy Head:

> And with slow swell the tide of morning bore
> Some blue swol'n cor'se to land; the pale recluse
> Dug in the chalk a sepulchre — above
> Where the dank sea-wrack mark'd the obsequies
> For the poor helpless stranger.
>
> (711–16)

The cavern in which the hermit has chosen to live is the result of the tide's hollowing of the chalky cliffs. The forces of the tide—like a predatory monster—eat their way into the "body" of the land (but also into the mind of the hermit), destroy formal integrity, and will ultimately bring about a complete collapse. The cave is unstable and threatened by the forces of wind and water, and so:

> One dark night
> The equinoctial wind blew south by west,
> Fierce on the shore;—the bellowing cliffs were shook
> Even to their stony base, and fragments fell
> Flashing and thundering on the angry flood.
>
> (717–20)

This process of destruction not only affects the cliffs and the hermit's cavern, but it also demands the hermit's life. Instead of lamenting his death, however, Smith's speaker praises his search for an environment reflecting the state of his mind and life. Only in death has he found relief from his earthly grief and the bonds that still linked him with human existence; he has now entered a sphere that resembles the happiness that the lonely lovers' "ideal bliss" represents.

Unlike Smith's topical fragment which, in a very outspoken manner, reworks various strands of the mode of fragmentary in the eighteenth century, Wordsworth more subtly uses the poetics of association and allusiveness that the majority of writers of fragment texts employed. Oliver Elton long ago termed Wordsworth "the greatest inventor of poetical forms between Gray and Shelley,"[7] and Mary Jacobus and Stephen Parrish have demonstrated in detail the generic innovation that Wordsworth introduced with his poetry.[8]

In the prefatory note to "Tintern Abbey," Wordsworth is reluctant to classify the generic framework of the poem.[9] Although he relates it vaguely to the genre of the ode, he does not definitively attribute any generic rubric to his composition. He relies on the diffuseness of both the definition and the concept of the ode as an eighteenth-century poetic form and expression of the sublime—in short, on the Pindaric mode. In the prefatory note, Wordsworth refers to the "transitions" that are characteristic of the sublimity of the Pindaric ode. Kurt Schlüter considers the poem a production that ought to be understood as representing modal characteristics of the sublime ode. He notes, however, that Wordsworth does not structure his poem in accordance with the tripartite pattern of the classical hymn. The poet, Schlüter argues, may have tried to develop an alternative version of the genre that subscribed to his ideal of "a language of common man."[10]

Far from being a deliberate fragment, "Tintern Abbey" draws on features of eighteenth-century fragment modality and attempts to establish a sense of personal, as well as imaginative, experience, which employs strategies of associationism. Wordsworth uses the fragmentary as a mode that is indicative of human forgetting. Beth Lau notes that he "was aware of the fact that memories decay and his writing in many ways functioned as a means of suspending that process of deterioration."[11] Rather than offering a formally fragmented account of his perception of the abbey, Wordsworth's speaker introduces the past, which he defines in terms of fragmented memory and discrete spots of time, and the present, in which he combines the fragments of the past into recollections complete and perfect. The imperfect joys that he evokes are perfected by means of processes of concentration, association, and recollection. Out of personal experiences, Wordsworth creates an individuality that at the same time embodies his ideal of simple man. "Tintern Abbey," therefore, like the "lyrical" hermit of *Beachy Head*, provides a version of human memory, the process of recollection and fragmentation, and ultimately assumes the fugitive and fragmentary character of the Pindaric (m)ode. Wordsworth is traditional in his handling of the mode of the fragmentary and does not use the more radical form of the Romantic fragment poem, which D. F. Rauber defines as "temporary, something to be completed in time."[12]

Marjorie Levinson sheds light on Wordsworth's specific generic reference to the ode; to her, the main features of the ode are the "more general businesses of theme and procedure"[13] and not the transitions and the versification that Wordsworth has in mind. She describes this phenomenon of formal elusiveness as follows:

> "Tintern Abbey's" "wherefore" is, strictly, within the poem, strangely elusive. Its "whereby," consequently, assumes an independent interest and one that contains or engenders its own philosophic rationale. Most readers observe that an object does not materialize in the poem before it is effaced or smudged; a thought does not find full articulation before it is qualified or deconstructed: a point of view is not established before it dissolves into a series of impressions.[14]

Levinson characterizes the poem as a "fiction" and "a product of memory and desire."[15] In another sense, "Tintern Abbey" is a representation of Wordsworth's memory, the morphology of which, after five years, is a fragment that the poet, through recollection, attempts to integrate into a perfect whole. Mary Jacobus sees the poet's mind as a fragment in which the process of recollection concentrates the "beautifully controlled movement of the verse" with the "mood" of "tranquil restoration."[16] The recollective process is mobile and in constant flow, resisting definitive structural patterning, inasmuch as the "rhythms of thought — associative, exploratory, fluctuating in and out of the present" are expressive of the endlessness of reflection and introspective recall beyond the actual end of the poem.[17] Wordsworth's skill in representing the fragmentary character of his memory is reflected in what Coleridge sees as the poet's ability to "spread . . . the tone, the atmosphere and with it the depth and height of the ideal world, around forms, incidents and situations, for which the common view, custom had bedimmed all the lustre, had dried up the sparkle and the dew-drops."[18]

Intertextual references, as well as specific information such as the mention of Tintern Abbey, may serve as reference points that are not (or only fragmentarily) developed within the poem. The ruin of Tintern, therefore, is the ruin of the poet's memory of it. So, while most types of eighteenth-century poetic fragments attempt a representation of the aesthetic and ideological endeavor from fragmentariness to perfection, "Tintern Abbey" reverses this mode by starting with a very specific title, which then, instead of being more closely defined, is fragmented and, in Levinson's terms, "deconstructed" and dissolved into "a series of impressions"[19] in the poem itself. In other words, "the poem at once solves and conceals."[20]

Levinson's notion of the poem's "text-title incongruity" is thus also part of the paradox of the fragmentary, a paradox that found most striking expression in the mid-century rage for ruins and the diversified use of the fragmentary in many kinds of writing. What has been comprehended as a paradox in this study, Stuart Curran defines as the "continuing reversal both in the main argument and in its subterranean layers" of "the paradoxical record of the mind's desire for relief from contraries."[21] Wordsworth's paradox, in this regard, makes use of a "technique of displacement" by which the "beneficent oneness"[22] — which his mind vainly attempts to establish — is fragmented.

Wordsworth's poem is related to a kind of poetry that Anne Janowitz defines as "open-ended," representative of "the burden of incompletion," and "linked to the inexpressibility problem."[23] It is a literal and metaphorical ruin that reaches a state of completeness by means of the poet's attempt to achieve a synthesis of the various independent impressions that his mind collected on his first visit to the abbey. The ruins of Wordsworth's memory, however, do not "give . . . up poetic space to the shape of a fragment—the poetic incompletion, or part of a whole."[24] They use the mode of the fragmentary so typical of the Pindaric ode and celebrate Wordsworth's devotion to Nature, his attempt to return to a childhood state of mind when he can accept nature as a "guide" and "guardian." Ultimately, the fragmentary inspires Wordsworth's imaginative memory, permitting him "to develop and retain a unified identity that confirms [his] . . . implicit assumptions" about himself.[25]

Wordsworth, as Wolfgang Riehle suggests, "did not consider the fragment as a poetic problem."[26] Like many other proponents of the fragmentary mode in the eighteenth century, Wordsworth relies on strategies of fragmentation but foregrounds the importance of the imagination in his poem. While "Tintern Abbey" employs fragment modality, it still creates—through its use of association and the recollective imagination—a "convincing artistic whole although it transgresses strictly classical aesthetics."[27] Whereas *Beachy Head* contrasted architectural metaphors of the ruinous with the ruins of memory and past happiness, Wordsworth draws on the associations of the Pindaric ode to highlight his psychology of the fragmentary and his faith that the Eden that ode writers such as Collins longed for is in fact accessible through the powers of memory and the recollective imagination.

Epilogue

Although fragment modality evokes incompleteness and the unfinished, it paradoxically still aspires to evoke a sense of completeness or perfection. Eighteenth-century fragments usually refer to a greater framework such as the self, a community, or a work of literature (relating the fragmentary dynamically to an ideal view of holistic universality and integrity), so that a sense of completion can be inferred. Romantic period poems such as *Beachy Head* and "Tintern Abbey," by contrast, deploy a (subjectified) form that is, at times, highly personal, incomplete, and requires the reader to apprehend its finality. Richard Terry notes the significance of associationism and argues that it "allowed poetry to be conceived as pre-eminently concerned with the coining of original and unlikely conjunctions between things."[1] Associations established connections between otherwise disjunctive, fragmentary, and unrelated elements, and thereby created an original or symbolic sense of unity that was not inherent in the independent parts. Any passage could be related to another—as in *The Seasons*—and although this liberty of form was not accepted without debate, the importance of association—especially by writers of long-poems—was soon recognized.

In *The Daring Muse*, Margaret Anne Doody has provided the most sustained treatment of generic dissociation in the eighteenth century; she refrains, however, from using the term "fragment" to denote a generic and modal concept that developed prominently in the period. She writes more generally of the "Restoration-Augustan task of exploding genres,"[2] noting that the "new poet had to face the job of creating each poem as its own genre, anticipating within it the mockery or subversion of any of the styles it employed."[3] It is dangerous to interpret changes that were introduced to form, modes, and generic concepts exclusively in terms of "mockery" and "subversion," since that would entail reducing the poetic production of the fragment to merely a reaction to already existing forms. Rather than understanding the fragmentary mode in this limited and limiting way, it should be understood as a

136

mode of expression that was appropriated by poets and made to fit such contexts as satire, impromptus, long-poems, literary fakes, and anthologized literature: it developed as a transgeneric mode in the eighteenth century. In its numerous manifestations, the fragmentary attempts to construct or recover contexts. Susan Stewart points out:

> Verbal art was collected artifactually since the sixteenth century for a number of reasons: to establish a corpus of texts that would reflect nationalist impulses and hence lend validity to a vernacular heritage in contradistinction to a classical one; to "rescue" forms that seemed to be disappearing—i.e., to effect a kind of archaeology of speech forms parallel to the rescue of what is properly known as "material" culture; to place such "specimens" as curiosities, characterized by fragmentation and exoticism, against the contemporary and so use them to establish the parameters of the present.[4]

The past, in its recovered state, was considered valuable, and through this valuing of the past the fragmentary (inherent in its representation) was legitimized. K. K. Ruthven observes, in this regard, that "Chatterton's 'Rowley' poems, Macphossian and the ballad revival are all examples of 'distressed genres', the formula for which is 'a counterfeit materiality and an authentic nostalgia'."[5]

The contention of this book has been that there is a need to readjust the literary-historical account of modes and forms in the eighteenth century by means of a consideration of the mode of the fragmentary. As such, it joins the revisionist work of recent decades that, in Christine Gerrard's words, has helped to "transform eighteenth-century poetry from an orderly, harmonious, and slightly dull field for humanist enquiry into a constantly surprising, sometimes unstable world in which such preoccupations as pain, pleasure, power, and metamorphosis exerted a powerful hold on the poetic imagination."[6] It has countered more traditional scholarship focusing on the emergence of the fragment in the Romantic period, arguing implicitly for a reconsideration of the still prevalent periodization model of classic versus Romantic. In that respect, the eighteenth-century fragment is redefined as a more versatile and hybridized means of poetic expression that is more complex and varied in both method and subject matter (because more diverse, as it invents itself with each poem) than its Romantic equivalent. While noting a number of correspondences with later fragments, this account has also introduced a range of ideas that provide stimuli for further research into eighteenth-century modes and kinds, especially in as far as it has introduced little known works of poetry that strongly evidence the utilization of the fragmentary.

Instead of comprehending the various transgeneric manifestations of the fragment as part of a dialectic, they ought to be regarded as different occurrences of the same phenomenon, conditioned by the numerous different aesthetic, ideational, and cultural trends at work at the time. Consequently, the mode of the fragmentary in the eighteenth century is more heterogeneous and polymorphous than its Romantic equivalent; this account demonstrates that forms such as the ode, the ballad and song, the long-poem, and many more integrated features of the incomplete and unfinished in their poetic practice and thereby helped to legitimize a mode that has become of central importance to the modern reader of texts such as Joyce's *Ulysses*. Gert Ueding's contention that the fragmentary work is no longer a completed result, which has absorbed the various stages of its making, but remains an intermediate stage on its way to an approach toward a never-to-be reached idea of a union of innumerable diffuse elements, needs to be reconsidered in the light of my study.[7] His suggestion is only applicable to the Romantic notion of a fragment as a representation of the "progressus ad infinitum."[8] The use of the poetic fragment in the eighteenth century, unlike the fragment tradition of the nineteenth century, draws on the inherent generic tensions that genres like the epic, the long-poem, or the ode offer to the poet, while, at the same time, poets of that period theorize these unfinished and fragmentary compositions within a context of the originality and the perfection of sublime "Pindaric" genius. Therefore, the analysis of the fragment in the eighteenth century is more than an examination of a marginal phenomenon in the context of form and genre: it is an investigation of an important mode in literary history and a central stage in the legitimization and popularization of the fragment when various strands of poetic conceptualizations of the poetic of the unfinished were combined with one another, counteracted each other, or developed side by side.

Notes

Chapter 1. Fragment Modality

1. Paula R. Backscheider, *Eighteenth-Century Women Poets: Inventing Agency, Inventing Genre* (Baltimore: The Johns Hopkins University Press, 2005), xxi.

2. G. Gabrielle Starr, *Lyric Generations: Poetry and the Novel in the Long Eighteenth Century* (Baltimore: The Johns Hopkins University Press, 2004), 2.

3. Starr, *Lyric Generations*, 1.

4. Ibid., 2, 6.

5. Jennifer Keith, *Poetry and the Feminine: From Behn to Cowper* (Newark: University of Delaware Press, 2005), 11, 15.

6. See Dustin Griffin, *Patriotism and Poetry in Eighteenth-Century Britain* (Cambridge: Cambridge University Press, 2002); Suvir Kaul, *Poems of Nation, Anthems of Empire: English Verse in the Long Eighteenth Century* (Charlottesville, Va.: University Press of Virginia, 2000); Donna Landry, *The Muses of Resistance: Laboring-class Women's Poetry in Britain, 1739–1796* (Cambridge: Cambridge University Press, 1990), and William Christmas, *The Lab'ring Muses: Work, Writing, and Social Order in English Plebeian Poetry, 1730–1830* (Newark: University of Delaware Press, 2001).

7. Eric Rothstein, *Restoration and Eighteenth-Century Poetry, 1660–1780* (Boston: Routledge & Kegan Paul, 1981), 99.

8. Christopher A. Strathman, *Romantic Poetry and the Fragmentary Imperative: Schlegel, Byron, Joyce, Blanchot* (New York: State University of New York Press, 2006), 1.

9. Howard Erskine-Hill, *The Augustan Idea in English Literature* (London: Edward Arnold, 1983), 247.

10. Elizabeth Wanning Harries, *The Unfinished Manner: Essays on the Fragment in the Later Eighteenth Century* (Charlottesville, Va.: University Press of Virginia, 1994), 13, 15.

11. Thomas McFarland, "Fragment Modalities and the Criteria of Romanticism," *Romanticism and the Forms of Ruin: Wordsworth, Coleridge, and Modalities of Fragmentation* (Princeton: Princeton University Press, 1981), 5. Oscar Kenshur, *Open Form and the Shape of Ideas: Literary Structures as Representations of Philosophical Concepts in the Seventeenth and Eighteenth Centuries* (Lewisburg: Bucknell University Press, 1986), 13, points out that "most scholars, and particularly those concerned with modern literature, apparently continue to adhere to the belief that discontinuous literary works—works whose gaps, whether logical, narrative, grammatical, or typographical, prevent the separate parts from combining into unified wholes—constitute a distinctly modern phenomenon that somehow reflects modern views about the world."

12. Marjorie Levinson, *The Romantic Fragment Poem: A Critique of a Form* (Chapel Hill: University of North Carolina Press, 1986), 59.

13. See John Beer, "Fragmentations and Ironies," *Questioning Romanticism*, ed. John Beer (Baltimore: The Johns Hopkins University Press, 1995), 234–64, as well as Lawrence Lipking, "The Genie in the Lamp: M. H. Abrams and the Motives of Literary History," *High Romantic Argument: Essays for M. H. Abrams*, ed. Lawrence Lipking (Ithaca: Cornell University Press, 1981), 128–48.

14. Alastair Fowler, *Kinds of Literature: An Introduction to the Theory of Genres and Modes* (Oxford: Clarendon Press, 1982), 60.

15. Ibid., 73.

16. This organic metaphor of birth is adopted from Jerome McGann. In *The Textual Condition*, Jerome McGann relativizes traditional ideas of generic openness or closure—fragmentariness or perfection—by noting that "perfection exists, but always within limits" (8). This qualifying statement makes it possible to reconsider the fragment as *one* representation of the "ceaseless process of textual development and mutation"—that is, a representation that is not inferior to genres that invite a sense of completeness and closure. According to McGann, no genre is "'universally' perfect; each displays perfection within a concrete set of determinants that have different spatial and temporal coordinates." See Jerome McGann, *The Textual Condition* (Princeton: Princeton University Press, 1991), 9, 9.

17. Camelia Elias, *The Fragment: Towards a History and Poetics of a Performative Genre* (Berne: Peter Lang, 2004), 1.

18. Fowler, *Kinds of Literature*, 56.

19. Klein, ed., *Shaftesbury's Characteristics*, x.

20. Ibid.

21. See Jerome McGann, *The Textual Condition* (Princeton: Princeton University Press, 1991).

22. Dryden's *Miscellany* (London: printed for J. Tonson, 1685), 169–72, contained a fragment entitled "Part of Virgil's fourth Georgick, English'd by the E. of M."

23. Barbara M. Benedict, "Publishing and reading poetry," *The Cambridge Companion to Eighteenth-Century Poetry*, ed. John Sitter (Cambridge: Cambridge University Press, 2001), 68. Benedict further notes: "As public vehicles of poetic unity, miscellanies manifested the connection between writers in print. These compilations of verse thus helped to establish ideological and aesthetic schools of verse. At the same time, they also encouraged readers to compare and rank authors and works."

24. Ibid., 68, notes that publishers, instead of publishing single poems, preferred the publication of "plentiful miscellanies that contained excerpts and patches from longer works, mingled with a variety of short, light, extemporaneous verse." More specialized works like translations were mostly published by subscription.

25. I would like to express my gratitude to Heather Larmour for discussing "Beauties" anthologies with me and for sharing her unpublished research. See Heather Larmour, "Anthologising the Author in the Eighteenth-Century 'Beauties' Tradition" (unpublished doctoral thesis, University of Liverpool, 2002). "Beauties" anthologies such as *Thesaurus Dramaticus* (1724, republished as *The Beauties of the English Stage* [1737]), *The Beauties of the Spectators, Tatlers and Guardians* (1753), *The Beauties of English Prose* (1772), and *The Beauties of Biography* (1777) enjoyed great popularity. See also Barbara M. Benedict, "The 'Beauties' of Literature, 1750–1820: Tasteful Prose and Fine

Rhyme for Private Consumption," *1660–1850: Ideas, Aesthetics, and Inquiries in the Early Modern Period*, 1 (1994), 317–46.

26. *Lady's Poetical Magazine* (London: printed for Harrison, 1781), no pagination.

27. *The Beauties of Sterne* (Dublin: printed for W. Wilson, 1784), 3.

28. Ibid., 5.

29. Ibid. "The chaste part of the world complained so loudly of the obscenity which taints the writings of Sterne . . . , that those readers under their immediate inspection were not suffered to penetrate beyond the title-page of his *Tristram Shandy*."

30. Larmour, "Anthologising the Author in the Eighteenth-Century 'Beauties' Tradition," 123.

31. Ibid., 124.

32. Ibid., 123.

33. Benedict, "Publishing and reading poetry," 68.

34. Edward Young, *Conjectures on Original Composition* (Leeds: Scolar Press, 1966), 12.

35. Ibid., 17. Later on he notes that "[t]oo great Awe for them [the Wits] lays Genius under restraint, and denies it that free scope, that full elbow-room, which is requisite for striking its most masterly strokes. Genius is a Master-workman, Learning is but an Instrument" (Young, *Conjectures on Original Composition*, 25). See also Rudolf Sühnel, "Tradition und Originalgenie: Bemerkungen zu Edward Youngs *Conjectures on Original Composition*," *Geschichtlichkeit und Neuanfang im sprachlichen Kunstwerk: Studien zur englischen Philologie zu Ehren von Fritz W. Schulze*, ed. W. G. Müller and Peter Erlebach (Tübingen: Narr, 1981), 163–67.

36. Young, *Conjectures on Original Composition*, 55.

37. John Dennis, *The Grounds of Criticism in Poetry* (London: Geo. Strahan, 1704), 20–21.

38. Arthur Johnston, "Poetry and Criticism after 1740," *Dryden to Johnson*, ed. Roger Lonsdale, The Penguin History of Literature (Harmondsworth: Penguin, 1993), 315.

39. Alexander Pope, "Preface to the *Iliad*," *The Iliad of Homer*, ed. Maynard Mack, The Twickenham Edition of the Works of Alexander Pope (London: Methuen and New Haven: Yale University Press, 1967), 3.

40. *Poetical Dictionary, or, the Beauties of English Poets*, 4 vols (London: Newbery, 1761), 1: v.

41. *Boeoticorum Liber: or a New Art of Poetry. Containing the best Receipt for making all Sorts of Poems. According to the Modern Taste* (Dublin, no date), 10.

42. *Hardyknute: A Fragment. Being the First Canto of an Epick Poem; With General Remarks and Notes* (London: R. Dodsley, 1740), 9, 4.

43. *Hardyknute*, 4.

44. William Bowman Piper, *The Heroic Couplet* (Cleveland: Press of Case Western Reserve University, 1969), 6. Earlier George Saintsbury, *The Peace of the Augustans: A Survey of Eighteenth-Century Literature as a Place of Rest and Refreshment* (London: G. Bell, 1916), 5, had noted the ambivalence of poetic and metrical freedom, as well as the closure entailed by the couplet: "Dryden . . . had shown exceptional proficiency in many kinds of metre, but he had principally devoted himself to one—the stopped heroic couplet, which is perhaps more traceable to the final distichs of Fairfax's octave in his Tasso than to anything else, just as the original couplet of Chaucer was probably determined by his own not diminutive practice in the Troilus. Dryden, however, while

presenting an immense improvement on Sandys, Sir John Beaumont, the much praised Waller, and Cowley, had too much of the divine freedom and variety of poetry in him to follow up the idées mères of this couplet — 'smoothness' and 'correctness' at all slavishly or even quite faithfully."

45. Doody, *The Daring Muse*, 258.

46. According to J. Paul Hunter, the "arrangement [of text] on the page becomes a set of directions related to meaning and response; the emphasis is on seeing the poem as a conscious work of art that employs words and syntax toward a progressive, cumulative, reflective end. Poems, arranged in stanzas, or paragraph blocks, look as if they move consciously from one more or less symmetrical shape to another toward some kind of end result, and that is in fact what they mean to do. Even the way the lines end — with a conscious stopping at the end of a certain number of syllables — suggests visually the way the poem structures meaning; . . . clauses and sentences are proceeding rationally, cumulatively, and progressively toward some end." See J. Paul Hunter, "Couplets and Conversation," *The Cambridge Companion to Eighteenth-Century Poetry*, ed. John Sitter (Cambridge: Cambridge University Press, 2001), 21.

47. Eric Rothstein, *Restoration and Eighteenth-Century Poetry, 1660–1780* (London: Routledge & Kegan Paul, 1981), 61.

48. Wolfgang Riehle, specifying the mode of the fragmentary in Coleridge's "Kubla Khan," argues that the poet's imagination "with its power of creating new poetic visions is sometimes stronger and more intense than his ability to give this poetic vision . . . form and shape so that the result is inevitably a mere fragment." See Wolfgang Riehle, "The Fragment in English Romantic Poetry," *Classical Models in Literature*, ed. Zoran Konstantinovic, Warren Anderson, and Walter Dietze (Innsbruck: Institut für Sprachwissenschaft der Universität Innsbruck, 1979), 136.

CHAPTER 2. THE "PINDARIC" MODE

1. Sophie Thomas, "The Fragment," *Romanticism: An Oxford Guide*, ed. Nicholas Roe (Oxford: Oxford University Press, 2004), 512, 507.

2. Annamaria Sportelli, "Sublimity and Fragmentariness: Forms and Discourse," *La Questione Romantica*, 10 (2001), 59.

3. Eighteenth-century textual scholarship contributed significantly to legitimizing the fragment, as fragmentary texts were translated, commented on, and made available to readers whose sense of genre had been defined by the prescriptivist ideals of French classicism. In the introduction to her edition of Epictetus, Elizabeth Carter defends the fragmentary nature of the text: "Very little Order or Method is to be found in them [the fragments of Epictetus], or was from the Nature of them to be expected. The Connexion is often scarcely discoverable: a Reference to particular Incidents, long since forgotten, at the same time that it evidences their Genuineness, often renders them obscure in some Places; and the great Corruption of the Text, in others. Yet, under all these Disadvantages, this immethodical Collection is perhaps one of the most valuable Remains of Antiquity; and they, who consult it with any Degree of Attention, can scarcely fail of receiving Improvement." See Elizabeth Carter, ed., *The Works of Epictetus, Consisting of His Discourses, in Four Books, Preserved by Arrian, 'The Enchiridion', and Fragments*, 2 vols (London: printed for F. C. and J. Rivington, 1807), 1: xl–xli.

4. L. C. Martin, ed., *Abraham Cowley: Poetry and Prose* (Oxford: Clarendon Press, 1949), xv–xxxix, xxvi.

5. Ibid., 74.

6. Ibid., xxvi.

7. Ibid., 38.

8. Thomas Parnell, *An Essay on the Different Stiles of Poetry* (Dublin: Edward Sandys, 1715), 14.

9. John Dennis, *The Grounds of Criticism in Poetry* (London: Geo. Strahan, 1704), 5.

10. Joseph Addison, *The Spectator*, ed. Donald F. Bond (Oxford: Clarendon Press, 1965). See also Rudolf Sühnel, *Der Park als Gesamtkunstwerk des englischen Klassizismus am Beispiel von Stourhead* (Heidelberg: Carl Winter Universitätsverlag, 1977), 14–15.

11. Margaret Anne Doody, *The Daring Muse: Augustan Poetry Reconsidered* (Cambridge: Cambridge University Press, 1985), 250.

12. Charles Gildon, *The Complete Art of Poetry*, 2 vols (London: Charles Rivington, 1718), 1: 180.

13. Penelope Wilson, "'High Pindaricks upon stilts': A Case-Study in the Eighteenth-Century Classical Tradition," *Rediscovering Hellenism: The Hellenic Heritage and the English Imagination*, ed. G. W. Clarke and J. C. Eade (Cambridge: Cambridge University Press, 1989), 28.

14. Gildon, *The Complete Art of Poetry*, 1: 179.

15. Ibi., 1: 180.

16. John Ogilvie, *An Essay on the Lyric Poetry of the Ancients*, introduced by Wallace Jackson, Augustan Reprint Society Publication, No. 139 (Los Angeles: Augustan Reprint Society, 1970), xiii.

17. In 1762, John Ogilvie, "Essay on the Lyric Poetry of the Ancients," *Poems on Several Subjects* (London: R. Dodsley, 1762), xxiv, characterized the ode by the following: "While the other branches of Poetry have been gradually modelled by the rules of criticism, the Ode hath only been hanged in a few external circumstances, and the enthusiasm, obscurity and exuberance which characterised it when first introduced, continue to be ranked among its capital and discriminating excellencies."

18. Edward Young, *Ocean. An Ode* (London: printed for Tho. Worrall, 1728), 18–19.

19. Ibid., 20. Young makes clear, however, that Pindar's apparent madness is sublimely and divinely inspired, but that it is never devoid of a logic of its own: "*Pindar*, who has as much Logick at the bottom, as *Aristotle* or *Euclid*, to some Criticks has appear'd as mad; and must appear so to all, who enjoy no portion of his own divine Spirit. Dwarf-understandings, measuring Others by their own standard, are apt to think they see a Monster, when they see a Man" (20).

20. Ibid., 23, 21.

21. Ibid., *Ocean*, 26–27.

22. *Odes (by "Mr Barnett")* (no place of publication, 1760). This is the copy of the Beinecke Rare Books and Manuscript Library, Yale University. Call number: Ib59 T766P.

23. Richard Shepherd, *Odes Descriptive and Allegorical* (London: printed for M. Cooper, 1761), iv. See also, James Scott, *Odes on several subjects* (Cambridge: printed by J. Bentham, 1761), 5.

24. Henry Pemberton, *Observations on Poetry, Especially the Epic, Occasioned by the late Poem upon Leonidas* (London: H. Woodfall, 1738), 100.

25. William Wordsworth, "Preface to *Lyrical Ballads*," *William Wordsworth*, ed. Carlos Baker (New York: Holt, 1954), 114.

26. Pemberton, *Observations on Poetry, Especially the Epic, Occasioned by the late Poem upon Leonidas*, 134.

27. "Advertisement," *Escapes of a Poetical Genius* (London: Marshall Sheepey, 1752), no pagination.

28. Hugh Blair, *Lectures on Rhetoric and Belles Lettres* (London: T. Cadell, 1785), 125.

29. Daniel Webb, *Remarks on the Beauties of Poetry* (London: printed for R. and J. Dodsley, 1762), 5.

30. Lisa M. Steinman, *Masters of Repetition: Poetry, Culture, and Work in Thomson, Wordsworth, Shelley, and Emerson* (Basingstoke: Macmillan, 1998), 9–12.

31. The trend of publishing "fugitive poetry" (meaning publications that actually had the word "fugitive" in the title) started prominently in the late 1750s. Some examples are Horace Walpole, *Fugitive Pieces in Verse and Prose* (Strawberry Hill: Strawberry Hill Press, 1758); *Fugitive Pieces on Various Subjects. By Several Authors*, 2 vols. (London: R. and J. Dodsley, 1761); *Real Characters, and Genuine Anecdotes, political, polite, gallant, theatrical, intriguing, prudish . . . interspersed with some fugitive miscellaneous pieces of the best modern authors and poets* (London: W. Bingley, 1769); J. Almon, *The Fugitive Miscellany*, 2 vols. (London: J. Almon, 1774); The Reverend John Moir, ed., *Gleanings; or, Fugitive Pieces [in prose and verse]*, 2 vols. (London: printed for the Author, 1785); *The Literary Miscellany; or, Elegant Selections of the Most Admired Fugitive Pieces, and Extracts from Works of the Greatest Merit: with Originals; in prose and verse* (Manchester: printed by G. Nicholson, 1794). The majority of "fugitive" publications, however, appear after 1790 and reach a climax in the nineteenth century.

32. Nick Groom, "Fragments, Reliques, and MSS: Chatterton and Percy," *Thomas Chatterton and Romantic Culture*, ed. Nick Groom (Basingstoke: Macmillan, 1999), 3.

33. Robert Dodsley, *The Art of Poetry* (London: R. Dodsley, 1741), 2.

34. Leonard Welsted, *Epistles, Odes, etc. Written on Several Subjects with a Dissertation Concerning the Perfection of the English Language, the State of Poetry, etc.* (London: J. Walthoe, 1725), xv.

35. *Odes of Pindar, with several other Pieces in Prose and Verse, translated from the Greek by Gilbert West* (London: printed for R. Dodsley, 1749), no pagination.

36. Ibid.

37. Ibid.

38. Ibid.

39. Ibid.

40. John Dryden, juxtaposing Greek and Roman styles in the "Preface" to *Fables Ancient and Modern* (1700), had already noted that "Virgil was of a quiet, sedate Temper; Homer was violent, impetuous, and full of Fire. The chief Talent of Virgil was Propriety of Thoughts, and Ornament of Words: Homer was rapid in his Thoughts, and took all the Liberties both of Numbers, and of Expressions, which his Language, and the Age in which he liv'd allow'd him: Homer's Invention was more copious, Virgil's more confin'd." John Dryden, "Preface to *Fables Ancient and Modern*," *The Poems and Fables of John Dryden*, ed. James Kinsley (Oxford: Oxford University Press, 1961), 524. Dryden's characterization of Homer in the terms that Longinus had used for the sublime—that is, "violent, impetuous, and full of Fire"—is expressive of his

awareness that Greek writing was not always rigidly adhering to rules of exactness and prescriptiveness but allowed "Liberties both of Numbers, and of Expressions."

41. Ralph Cohen, "The Return to the Ode," *The Cambridge Companion to Eighteenth-Century Poetry*, ed. John Sitter (Cambridge: Cambridge University Press, 2001), 208.

42. Robert Mayo, "The Contemporaneity of the *Lyrical Ballads*," *PMLA* 69 (1954), 506.

43. Nathanial Teich, "The Ode in English Literary History: Transformations from the Mid-Eighteenth to the Early Nineteenth Century," *Papers on Language and Literature* 21 (1985), 94.

44. Fry, *The Poet's Calling in the English Ode*, 4–5.

45. See Kurt Schlüter, *Die Englische Ode: Studien zu ihrer Entwicklung unter Einfluß der antiken Hymne* (Bonn: Bouvier, 1964).

46. William Hamilton, *Poems on Several Occasions* (Edinburgh: printed for W. Gordon, 1760), 101–2. See also Nelson S. Bushnell, *William Hamilton of Bangour, Poet and Jacobite* (Aberdeen: Aberdeen University Press, 1957).

47. Murray G. H. Pittock, *Poetry and Jacobite Politics in Eighteenth-Century Britain and Ireland* (Cambridge: Cambridge University Press, 1994), 173, 174.

48. David Mallet, "A Fragment," *The Union: or Select Scots and English Poems*, ed. Thomas Warton (Edinburgh [actually printed in Oxford]: printed for the Author, 1753), 24–27.

49. David Nichol Smith, "Thomas Warton's Miscellany: *The Union*," *Review of English Studies* 19, no. 75 (1943): 270.

50. James Mulholland, "Gray's Ambition: Printed Voices and Performing Bards in the Later Poetry," *ELH* 75 (2008): 110.

51. Mulholland, "Gray's Ambition," 125.

52. Levinson, *The Romantic Fragment Poem*, 56.

53. Shaun Irlam, *Elations: The Poetics of Enthusiasm in Eighteenth-Century Britain* (Stanford, Calif.: Stanford University Press, 1999), 65.

54. Leslie Earl Griggs, ed., *Collected Letters of Samuel Taylor Coleridge*, 6 vols. (Oxford: Clarendon Press, 1959–71), 1: 196.

55. Interleaved copy of the 1781 edition of Collins's poems, with John Langhorne's observations. Beinecke Rare Books and Manuscript Library, Yale University, Osborn Shelves c380. Cited by permission of the library.

56. Lonsdale, ed., *The Poems of Gray, Collins, and Goldsmith*, 434.

57. See Sandro Jung, "William Collins's 'Ode on the Poetical Character' and the 'cest of amplest power,'" *Neophilologus* 91, no. 2 (2007), 539–54.

58. John Sitter, *Literary Loneliness in Mid-Eighteenth-Century England* (Ithaca: Cornell University Press, 1982), 140.

59. Joseph Warton, *Odes on Various Subjects*, ed. Richard Wendorf (Los Angeles: Augustan Reprint Society, 1979).

60. *The Poetical Works of the Late Thomas Warton*, 2 vols. (Oxford: at the University Press, 1802), 2: 36–37.

61. Ibid., 1: 140.

62. James Scott, *Odes on Several Subjects* (Cambridge: printed by J. Bentham, 1761), 7.

63. See Sandro Jung, "Some Notes on William Mason and His Use of the 'Hymnal' Ode," *Studia Neophilologica* 76, no. 2 (2004), 176–81.

64. Casey Finch, "Immediacy in the *Odes* of William Collins," *Eighteenth-Century Studies* 20 (1987): 286.

65. See Robin Dix, ed., *The Poetical Works of Mark Akenside* (Madison, N.J.: Fairleigh Dickinson University Press, 1996), 350–51.

66. The poem is cited from Lonsdale, ed., *The New Oxford Book of Eighteenth-Century Verse*, 312. E. Dower was experimenting with a number of genres but is nowadays practically unknown. His only publication of note is *The Salopian Esquire: or the Joyous Miller; a dramatick tale. To which are added, Poems* (London: printed for the author, 1739).

67. The text will be cited from Lonsdale, ed., 274.

68. William J. Christmas, *The Lab'ring Muses: Work, Writing, and the Social Order in English Plebeian Poetry, 1730–1830* (Newark: University of Delaware Press, 2001), 96.

69. Eric Partridge ed., *The Three Wartons: A Choice of Their Verse* (London: Scholartis Press, 1927), 54–55.

70. Ian Jack, *Augustan Satire: Intention and Idiom in English Poetry, 1660–1750* (Oxford: Clarendon Press, 1952), 146, comments on the variety of modes and forms of satire and says that the "term satire covers poems of many different sorts."

71. Myra Reynolds, ed., *The Poems of Anne, Countess of Winchilsea* (Chicago: University of Chicago Press, 1903), 142.

CHAPTER 3. INVENTING THE LONG-POEM

1. C. M. Bowra, *From Virgil to Milton* (London: Macmillan, 1945), 2.

2. Ibid. 3.

3. See Walter Jackson Bate, *The Burden of the Past and the English Poet* (Cambridge, Mass.: Harvard University Press, 1970).

4. David F. Gladish, ed., *Sir William Davenant's 'Gondibert'* (Oxford: Clarendon Press, 1971), 15–16. E. M. W. Tillyard, *English Epic and Its Background* (London: Chatto and Windus, 1954), 428, points out that *Gondibert*, rather than adopting a fashionable attitude toward the epic, is produced within a tradition that harks back to medieval compositions. According to Tillyard, it "is remote from the neo-classic austerity of form common in the *Davideis* and *Paradise Lost* . . . , and it is closer to the post-medieval arcadianisms of Sidney and D'Urfé and Chamberlayne" (428).

5. (London: printed for William Miller and Joseph Watts, 1685).

6. Walter J. Ong, *Orality and Literacy: The Technologizing of the Word* (London: Methuen, 1982), 19, 23.

7. Tillyard, *The English Epic and Its Background*, 422.

8. Ibid.

9. Ibid., 426.

10. Ibid., 426.

11. Martin, ed., *Abraham Cowley*, 33.

12. Timothy Dykstal, "The Epic Reticence of Abraham Cowley," *SEL* 31, no. 1 (1991), 103.

13. Ibid., 101.

14. Abraham Cowley, *Poems*, ed. A. R. Waller (Cambridge: Cambridge University Press, 1905), 12.

15. E. M. W. Tillyard, *The Epic Strain in the English Novel* (London: Chatto and Windus, 1958), 15.

16. Dykstal, "The Epic Reticence of Abraham Cowley," 96.

17. Ibid., 103.

18. In "The Resurrection," Cowley describes the effect of the "fierce" Pindaric force represented by Pegasus:

> Now praunces stately, and anon flies o're the place,
> Disdains the servile Law of any settled pace,
> Conscious and proud of his own natural force.

Cited from Martin, ed., *Abraham Cowley*, 49.

19. Ibid., 69.

20. Percival Stockdale, *Lectures on the Truly Eminent Poets*, 2 vols. (London: printed for the Author, 1807), 1: 2.

21. Ibid., 1: 16.

22. Ibid., 1: 19. "Spenser, in the texture of his fable, and in the minuter parts of his poem, commits capital faults, which are peculiarly his own. Instead of making his whole epopée a connected fable, each canto is, in fact, a distinct one" (1: 18).

23. Ibid., 1: 18–19.

24. Richard Hurd, *Moral and Political Dialogues; with Letters on Chivalry and Romance*, 3 vols. (London: printed for T. Cadell, 1788), 3: 266.

25. Ibid., 3: 266, 3: 267.

26. Ibid., 3: 268.

27. Ibid., 3: 268, 3: 272.

28. Ibid., 3: 272.

29. Ibid., 3: 275.

30. Patrick J. Cook, *Milton, Spenser and the Epic Tradition* (Aldershot: Ashgate, 1997), 99.

31. Thomas McFarland, *Romanticism and the Forms of Ruin: Wordsworth, Coleridge, and Modalities of Fragmentation* (Princeton: Princeton University Press, 1981), 11.

32. Cook, *Milton, Spenser and the Epic Tradition*, 135.

33. Tillyard, *English Epic and Its Background*, 434.

34. Tillyard, *English Epic and Its Background*, 434.

35. Mindele Anne Treip, *Allegorical Poetics and the Epic: The Renaissance Tradition to Paradise Lost* (Lexington: University Press of Kentucky, 1994), 80.

36. Ibid.

37. Ibid., 81.

38. Ault, ed., *Alexander Pope: Minor Poems*, 404.

39. Ibid., 404 n.

40. In contrast to Pope's rather fragmented beginning of *Brutus*, his translation of the *Iliad* starts coherently and rhapsodically with an invocation of the "heav'nly Goddess":

> Achilles' Wrath, to Greece the direful Spring
> Of Woes unnumber'd, heav'nly Goddess, sing!
> That Wrath which hurl'd to Pluto's gloomy Reign
> The Souls of mighty Chiefs untimely slain;

(1–4)

See Maynard Mack, ed., *Alexander Pope: The Iliad, Books I–IX*, 82.

41. The structural plan that Pope had designed for *Brutus* outlined a scheme to narrate episodic history. The various adventures and episodes of Brutus would then have been connected associatively by what Tasso termed the "verisimilar," but they must not distract attention from the wholeness and the supposedly *intact* (in the Aristotelian sense) structure of the epic. Apart from Pope's ambition to write an epic about Brutus in blank verse, he, by the age of fifteen, had produced some four thousand lines of an epic in couplets on Alcander, which, however, he was persuaded to destroy. See Dustin Griffin, "Milton and the Decline of Epic in the Eighteenth Century," *New Literary History* 14 (1982): 143–54; 145.

42. Griffin, "Milton and the Decline of Epic in the Eighteenth Century," 149.

43. Leo Damrosch, "Pope's Epic: What Happened to Narrative?," *The Eighteenth Century: Theory and Interpretation* 29, no. 2 (1988): 189–207; 195.

44. Damrosch, "Pope's Epic: What Happened to Narrative?," 197.

45. *Poems, by the Right Honourable the late Lord Lyttleton* (Aberdeen: printed for, and sold by, J. Boyle, 1777).

46. William Thompson, *Poems on Several Occasions, to which is added Gondibert and Birtha, a tragedy* (Oxford: printed at the Theatre, 1757), 28.

47. Henry Pemberton, *Observations on Poetry, Especially the Epic: Occasioned by the late poem upon Leonidas* (London: printed by H. Woodfall, 1738), 4.

48. Ibid., 9.

49. Richard Glover, *Leonidas. A Poem* (London: printed for R. Dodsley, 1738), iii, xxi.

50. Pemberton, *Observations on Poetry*, 10.

51. Ibid., 11.

52. *Monthly Review* 44 (1771): 341.

53. *Critical Review* 30 (1770): 381. See also *Critical Review*, 30 (1770): 379–80: "His august hero is strikingly characterized, and distinguished: we are interested in every word he speaks, in every motion of his majestick frame. Our minds accompany him attentively from the beginning of his march to his glorious death at Thermophylae. The portraits of his other heroes, and of the principal officers in Xerxes's army, are artfully, and strongly diversified."

54. *Critical Review* 30 (1770): 381.

55. John Ogilvie, *Rona: A Poem. In Seven Books* (London: printed for John Murray, 1777), xiii.

56. Samuel Johnson, "Life of Thomson," *The Lives of the Most Eminent English Poets; With Critical Observations on their Works*, ed. Roger Lonsdale (Oxford: Clarendon Press, 2006), 4: 104.

57. See, for instance, Sandro Jung, "Updating *Summer*, or Revising and Recomposing *The Seasons*," *On Second Thought: Updates in the Eighteenth Century*, ed. Elizabeth Kraft and Deborah Taylor Bourdeau (Newark: University of Delaware Press, 2007), 69–82.

58. John Dennis, *The Grounds of Criticism in Poetry* (London: Geo. Strahan, 1704), 24.

59. See Michael Cohen, "James Thomson and the Prescriptive Sublime," *The South Central Bulletin* 40, no. 4 (1980): 140.

60. Chalker, *The English Georgic: A Study in the Development of a Form* (London: Routledge & Kegan Paul, 1969), 133.

61. James Thomson, "Preface," *Winter: A Poem* (London: J. Millan, 1726), 15.

62. Johnson, "Life of Thomson," 3: 293.

63. Ralph Cohen, *The Art of Discrimination: Thomson's* The Seasons *and the Language of Criticism* (London: Routledge & Kegan Paul, 1964), 84. Stefanie Lethbridge, *James Thomson's Defence of Poetry: Intertextual Allusion in* The Seasons (Tübingen: Niemeyer, 2003), considers Thomson's use of intertextual allusion as a unifying device.

64. Shiels quoted in Cohen, *The Art of Discrimination*, 85.

65. Richard Terry, "Transitions and Digressions in the Eighteenth-Century Long Poem," *SEL* 32 (1992): 496. Terry further notes that there existed a very close relationship between "Beauties" anthologies and the practice of excerpting fragments of long-poems in these anthologies: "Many anthologies dubbed themselves as collections of poetic 'beauties,' and their existence as a means by which the disjected parts of long poems were offered to a wider reading public suggests how such poems were generally regarded as orchestrations of fragments" (496).

66. Johnson, "Life of Mallet," 4: 167, termed *The Excursion* "a desultory and capricious view of such scenes of Nature as his fancy led him, or his knowledge enabled him, to describe." Similarly, Johnson censures Richard Savage's *The Wanderer* in terms that are symptomatic of the structurally transgressive nature of the eighteenth-century long-poem.

67. John Brightland, *A Grammar of the English Tongue* (London, 1714), 138.

68. See Stefanie Lethbridge, "Anthological Reading Habits in the Eighteenth Century: The Case of Thomson's *Seasons*," *Anthologies of British Poetry: Critical Perspectives from Literary and Cultural Studies*, ed. Barbara Korte, Ralf Schneider, and Stephanie Lethbridge (Amsterdam: Rodopi, 2000), 89–103.

69. James Sambrook, *James Thomson, 1700–1748: A Life* (Oxford: Clarendon Press, 1991), 100. The disjunctive character of *The Seasons* is highlighted by Sambrook when he notes that "*Winter* is still twice as heavily punctuated as *Summer* and *Autumn*, and nearly three times as heavily as *Spring*. These relative levels of fluency could be seen as reflecting the poems' different subjects" (96). However, they might also indicate that there are indeed four different poems that are only fragments of Thomson's visions of a cycle of seasons.

70. Charles Peake, "Poetry 1700–1740," *Dryden to Johnson*, ed. Roger Lonsdale, The Penguin History of Literature (Harmondsworth: Penguin, 1993), 146, while not admitting the fragmentary character of the composition, has difficulty in maintaining his view of a general unity of the poem. According to him, "*The Seasons* contains passages of moralizing and philosophizing, but the unifying conception is that experience of nature can be inspiriting, uplifting and instructive."

71. John Aikin, "Life of Thomson," *The Seasons: Containing Spring, Summer, Autumn, Winter; by James Thomson: With His Last Corrections, Additions, and Improvements, with the life of the author: and An Essay on the Plan and Character of the Poem on The Seasons* (New York: Duyckinck, 1813), ix.

72. See Sandro Jung, "Epic, Ode, or Something New: The Blending of Genres in Thomson's *Spring*," *Papers on Language and Literature* 43, no. 2 (2007): 146–65.

73. Oscar Kenshur, *Open Form and the Shape of Ideas: Literary Structures as Representations of Philosophical Concepts in the Seventeenth and Eighteenth Centuries* (Lewisburg: Bucknell University Press, 1986), 71.

74. Ibid., 79.

75. Ibid., 78.

76. Ibid., 71.

77. Ibid., 88.

78. Ibid., 94.

79. Earl Miner, "From Narrative to 'Description' and 'Sense' in Eighteenth-Century Poetry," *SEL* 9, no. 3 (1969): 483.

80. Richard Jago, *Edge-Hill, A Poem* (London: J. Dodsley, 1767), vii.

81. David Mallet, *The Excursion. In Two Books* (London: J. Walthoe, 1728), 3.

82. (1: 345)

83. Ibid., iii–iv.

84. Barbara Kiefer Lewalski, "The Genres of *Paradise Lost*," *The Cambridge Companion to Milton*, ed. Dennis Danielson (Cambridge: Cambridge University Press, 1999), 115.

85. Isaac Watts, *Reliquiae Juveniles: Miscellaneous Thoughts in Verse and Prose* (London: Richard Ford, 1734), 320.

86. Ibid., 322.

87. Young, *Conjectures on Original Composition*, 60.

88. Ibid., 98.

89. Ibid., 58.

90. Johnson, "Life of Dyer," 4: 125.

91. Johnson, "Life of Thomson," 4: 104.

92. Arthur Johnston, "Poetry and Criticism after 1740," *Dryden to Johnson*, ed. Roger Lonsdale (Harmondsworth: Penguin, 1971, 1993), 340.

93. Edward Young, *Night Thoughts*, ed. Stephen Cornford (Cambridge: Cambridge University Press, 1989). The poem is cited from this edition.

94. Francis Fawkes and William Woty, eds., *The Poetical Calendar. Containing a collection of scarce and valuable pieces of poetry*, 12 vols. (London: printed by Dryden Leach, 1768), 8: 119.

95. Douglas Lane Patey, "Art and Integrity: Concepts of Self in Alexander Pope and Edward Young," *Modern Philology* 83, no. 4 (1986), 373.

96. Ibid., 374.

97. Ibid., 375.

98. See Barbara Kiefer Lewalski, Paradise Lost *and the Rhetoric of Literary Forms* (Princeton: Princeton University Press, 1985), Chapters 1 and 2. Lewalski's groundbreaking identification of modes and genres indicates ways in which eighteenth-century poets understood genres and modes and in how far they realized that renovation or intermodal structures and constructs—including the fragmentary—could effectively replace outmoded ones and represent an up-to-date version of Tillyard's notion of the "temper" of the age.

CHAPTER 4. "NEW" AND "AUTHENTIC" FRAGMENTS

1. Richard Terry, "Transitions and Digressions in the Eighteenth-Century Long Poem," *SEL* 32 (1992): 498.

2. See, for instance, W. Howard, *A Paraphrase in Verse, on part of the first book of Milton's* Paradise Lost (London: printed for the author, 1738), and *Spenser's Fairy Queen.*

Attempted in Blank Verse, with Notes, Critical and Explanatory (London: printed for T. and J. Egerton, 1783).

3. Raymond Dexter Havens, *The Influence of Milton on English Poetry* (New York: Russell and Russell, 1961), 35.

4. Marcus Walsh, *Shakespeare, Milton, and Eighteenth-Century Literary Editing* (Cambridge: Cambridge University Press, 1997), 54.

5. (London: G. Hawkins, 1739). The first eighteenth-century canto of *The Faerie Queene* was published as *An Original Canto of Spenser; design'd as part of his Fairy Queen, but never printed. Now made public [or rather written] by Nestor Ironside [Samuel Croxall]* (London, 1714), as well as *A New Canto of Spenser's Fairy Queen (by John Upton). Now first published* (London: G. Hawkins, 1747). In 1774, a blank-verse translation of Canto I was published as *Spencer's Fairy Queen, attempted in blank verse* (London: T. Davies, 1774).

6. "Thomas Gray to Richard West," *The Correspondence of Thomas Gray*, ed. Paget Toynbee and Leonard Whibley, 3 vols. (Oxford: Clarendon Press, 1935), 1: 170.

7. See Robert Dodsley, ed., *A Collection of Poems in Six Volumes by Several Hands* (London: R. and J. Dodsley, 1763), 2: 80–103.

8. Croxall, *An Original Canto of the Fairy Queen*, 3.

9. Ibid.

10. Ibid., 4.

11. Ibid.

12. Ibid., 6.

13. Earl R. Wasserman, *Elizabethan Poetry in the Eighteenth Century*, Illinois Studies in English Language and Literature (Urbana: University of Illinois Press, 1947), 107.

14. Christine Gerrard, "*The Castle of Indolence* and the Opposition to Walpole," *Review of English Studies* 41/161 (1990): 48, 49.

15. Gerrard, "*The Castle of Indolence* and the Opposition to Walpole," 49.

16. Wasserman, *Elizabethan Poetry in the Eighteenth Century*, 114.

17. H. E. Cory, *The Critics of Edmund Spenser* (Berkeley, Calif.: University of California Press, 1911), 82.

18. John Hughes, "Remarks on the *Fairy Queen*," *Eighteenth-Century Critical Essays*, ed. Scott Elledge, 2 vols (Ithaca: Cornell University Press, 1961), 1: 301.

19. Ibid., 304.

20. Addison, "*The Spectator* No. 183," 2: 45.

21. James Sambrook, ed., '*Liberty*'; '*The Castle of Indolence*', *and other poems* (Oxford: Clarendon Press, 1986). The poem is cited from this edition.

22. Thomson cited in Sambrook, *James Thomson*, 263.

23. Christine Gerrard, "*The Castle of Indolence* and the Opposition to Walpole," *Review of English Studies* 41 (1990): 46.

24. John Bancks, *Miscellaneous Works, in verse and prose, of John Bancks. Adorned with sculptures and illustrated with notes*, 2 vols. (London: printed by T. Aris, for the author, 1738), 1: vii.

25. Other texts, whether "minor epic poems" or long-poems, such as William Somerville's *The Chace* (1734), were understood as potentially being translations of an unknown book of Virgil's *Georgics*. In a letter dealing with *The Chace*, an unknown writer notes that on reading the poem, "I began to *fancy*, that another Georgic of Virgil, which had lain hid from the Learned for so many ages, had been brought to light,

& met with a translator of uncommon abilities." The text of the letter is reproduced in Sandro Jung, "An Unnoticed Account of William Somerville's *The Chace* (1734)," *Augustan Studies* 1 (2002), 102.

26. Anonymous, "Imitation of Spenser," *The Oxford Sausage*, 139.

27. The Reverend Joseph Sterling, *Poems* (London: printed for G. G. J. and J. Robinson, 1789), no pagination ["Cumbuscan; or, the Squire's Tale"].

28. Warton, ed., *The Oxford Sausage*, 109.

29. See Lady Elizabeth Halket Wardlow, *Hardyknute, a fragment of an antient Scots poem* (Glasgow: printed and sold by Robert Foulis, 1748).

30. See Mary Ellen Brown, "Old Singing Women and the Canon of Scottish Balladry and Song," *A History of Scottish Women's Writing*, ed. Douglas Gifford and Dorothy McMillan (Edinburgh: Edinburgh University Press, 1997), 44–57.

31. Mel Kersey, "Ballads, Britishness and *Hardyknute*, 1719–1859," Scottish *Studies Review* 5, no. 1 (2004): 50, 43.

32. *Hardyknute* (This printing does not give a place of publication or publisher), 4.

33. Ibid.

34. Ibid.

35. Ibid.

36. *Hardyknute*, 7.

37. Paget Toynbee and Leonard Whibley, eds., *The Correspondence of Thomas Gray*, 3 vols. (Oxford: Clarendon Press, 1971), 2: 665.

38. Thomas Percy, *Reliques of Ancient English Poetry, Collected by Thomas Percy, Bishop of Dromore* (London and Edinburgh: William P. Nimmo, 1881), 113.

39. Percy, *Reliques of Ancient English Poetry*, 280.

40. Roger Lonsdale, ed., *The Poems of Gray, Collins, and Goldsmith* (Harlow: Longman, 1969), 213.

41. Ibid.

42. Ibid., 216.

43. John Bancks, *Miscellaneous Works, in verse and prose*, 1: vi.

44. Thomas Percy, *Five Pieces of Runic Poetry, translated from the Icelandic language* (London: J. and R. Dodsley, 1763), no pagination.

45. Ibid.

46. Ibid.

47. Ibid.

48. Howard D. Weinbrot, *Britannia's Issue: The Rise of British Literature from Dryden to Ossian* (Cambridge: Cambridge University Press, 1993), 529.

49. Fiona F. Stafford, *The Sublime Savage: A Study of James Macpherson and* The Poems of Ossian (Edinburgh: Edinburgh University Press, 1988), 101, 102.

50. (London: printed for S. Hooper, 1765).

51. This poem was included in *A Collection of Original Poems, by the Rev. Mr Blacklock, and other Scotch Gentlemen* (Edinburgh: printed for A. Donaldson, 1760).

52. On the question of originality and Ossian, see Andreas Höfele, "Die Originalität der Fälschung: zur Funktion des literarischen Betrugs in England, 1750–1800," *Poetica* 18 (1986): 75–95; R. B. Fitzgerald, "The Style of Ossian," *Studies in Romanticism* 6 (1966): 22–33, and most comprehensively, Daffyd Moore, *Enlightenment and Romance in James Macpherson's* The Poems of Ossian: *Myth, Genre, and Cultural Change* (Aldershot: Ashgate, 2003).

53. For the idea of forgery as history, see Ian Haywood, "The Making of History: Historiography and Literary Forgery in the Eighteenth Century," *Literature and History* 9 (1983): 139–57.

54. On the influence of Ossian on other writers, see Michael MacCraith, "Charlotte Brooke and James MacPherson," *Litteraria Pragensia* 10 (2000): 5–17.

55. "Thomas Gray to William Mason," *The Correspondence of Thomas Gray*, 2: 694–95.

56. Paul Baines, *The House of Forgery in Eighteenth-Century Britain* (Aldershot: Ashgate, 1999), 103.

57. See Hugh Blair, *A Critical Dissertation on the Poems of Ossian, the Son of Fingal* (London: printed for T. Beckett and P. A. De Hondt, 1763).

58. David Dalrymple writing to Horace Walpole, cited in Baines, *The House of Forgery in Eighteenth-Century Britain*, 104.

59. Ibid.

60. W. J. Courthope, *A History of English Poetry* (London: Macmillan, 1905), 5: 400.

61. James Macpherson, *Fragments of Ancient Poetry* (Edinburgh: G. Hamilton and J. Balfour, 1760), iii.

62. Ibid., iv–v; v.

63. Paget Toynbee, ed., *The Letters of Horace Walpole, Fourth Earl of Orford* (Oxford: Clarendon Press, 1903), 4: 349.

64. Charlotte Brooke, *Reliques of Irish Poetry* (Dublin: George Bonham, 1789), vi: "I am aware that in the following there will sometimes be found a sameness, and repetition of thought, appearing but too plainly in the English version, though scarcely perceivable in the original Irish, so great is the variety as well as beauty peculiar to that language."

65. Thomas Chatterton, *The Complete Works of Thomas Chatterton*, ed. Donald S. Taylor and Benjamin B. Hoover, 2 vols. (Oxford: Clarendon Press, 1971), 1: 645.

66. Nick Groom, "Literature, 1757–1776," *A Companion to Literature from Milton to Blake*, ed. David Womersley (Oxford: Blackwell, 2000), 479. Groom notes that "Chatterton composed in a stunning array of styles and voices—elegies, Churchillian satire, political letters, African eclogues, Saxon Ossianics, and medieval verse—and under many different pseudonyms" (278).

67. For an excellent reading of the "Balade," see Fritz Willy Schulze, "An Excelente Balade of Charitie," *Versdichtung der englischen Romantik: Interpretationen*, ed. Teut A. Riese and Dieter Riesner (Berlin: Erich Schmidt Verlag, 1968), 45–64. Also, Ian Haywood, "Chatterton's Plans for the Publication of the Forgery," *RES* 36/141 (1985): 58–68.

68. Nick Groom, ed., *Thomas Chatterton: Selected Poems* (Cheltenham: Cyder Press, 2003), vi.

CHAPTER 5. RUINS

1. Balachandra Rajan, *The Form of the Unfinished: English Poetics from Spenser to Pound* (Princeton: Princeton University Press, 1985), 3.

2. Ibid.

3. Jennifer Snead, "*Disjecta Membra Poetae*: The Aesthetics of the Fragment and Johnson's Biographical Practice in the *Lives of the English Poets*," *The Age of Johnson: A*

Scholarly Annual 15 (2004): 37. Snead notes that "the affective power and aesthetic pleasure of the fragment lies in the fact of it being just that: a part, not a whole" (38).

4. For the growing awareness of eighteenth-century Hellenism, see the excellent account by John Buxton, *The Grecian Taste: Literature in the Age of Neo-classicism, 1740– 1820* (London: Macmillan, 1978), 1–24. The interest in ruins, manifested in expensively printed volumes of plates, started at the beginning of the century with the publication of *The Antiquities of Palmyra* (1705).

5. Robert Wood, *The Ruins of Palmyra, otherwise Tedmor in the desart* (London: printed for R. Dodsley, 1753), 15.

6. Edmund Burke, *On the Sublime* (New York: P. F. Collier & Son, 1909), 68.

7. Burke, *On the Sublime*, 69.

8. Ibid., 97.

9. Sophie Thomas, "The Fragment," *Romanticism: An Oxford Guide*, ed. Nicholas Roe (Oxford: Oxford University Press, 2004), 504.

10. See Kelvin Everest, "Ozymandias: The Text in Time," *Essays and Studies: Percy Bysshe Shelley*, ed. Kelvin Everest (Cambridge: Brewer, 1992), 30: "The ruin of Ozymandias has a generic kind of significance that is deeply typical of a whole category of human experience and behaviour."

11. Anne Janowitz, *England's Ruins: Poetic Purpose and the National Landscape* (Oxford: Blackwell, 1990), 4.

12. Ibid., 5.

13. Ibid., 13.

14. Samuel Johnson, "Life of Shenstone," *Lives of the Most Eminent English Poets; with Critical Observations on their Works*, ed. Roger Lonsdale (Oxford: Clarendon Press, 2006), 4: 127.

15. *Select Works of William Shenstone* (Edinburgh: printed for T. Balfour and W. Creech, 1773), 106.

16. Shenstone, "Unconnected Thoughts on Gardening," 110.

17. A. R. Humphreys, *William Shenstone: An Eighteenth-Century Portrait* (Cambridge: Cambridge University Press, 1937), 46.

18. Shenstone, "Unconnected Thoughts on Gardening," 114.

19. Elizabeth Wanning Harries, *The Unfinished Manner: Essays on the Fragment in the Later Eighteenth Century* (Charlottesville: University Press of Virginia, 1994), 71.

20. Harries, *The Unfinished Manner*, 71.

21. Thomas McFarland, *Romanticism and the Forms of Ruin: Wordsworth, Coleridge, and Modalities of Fragmentation* (Princeton: Princeton University Press, 1981), 19.

22. Harries, *The Unfinished Manner*, 72.

23. Ibid., 84.

24. Ibid., 85.

25. Any reference will be to the version reproduced in J. C. Smith and Ernest de Sélincourt, eds., *Spenser: Poetical Works* (Oxford: Oxford University Press, 1970), 470–78.

26. Johnson, "Life of Mallet," 4: 167.

27. See Belinda Humfrey, *John Dyer* (Cardiff: University of Wales Press, 1980), 47–57.

28. See E. W. Pitcher, "Eighteenth-Century Gothic Fragments and the Paradigm of Violation and Despair," *Studies in Short Fiction* 33 (1996): 35–42.

29. William Gilpin, *Observations on the River Wye*, ed. Sutherland Lyall (Richmond: Richmond Publishing, 1973), 59.

30. Richard C. Boys, ed., *"Grongar Hill" by John Dyer* (Baltimore: Johns Hopkins University Press, 1941). The poem is cited from this edition.

31. For comparative analyses of the two variants of "Grongar Hill," see Sandro Jung, *"Forming Thought and Feasting Sense": The Great Compositions of John Dyer* (Trier: WVT, 2000), 4–34, and Garland Greever, "The Two Versions of *Grongar Hill*," *JEGP* 16 (1917): 274–81.

32. Stuart Piggot, *Ruins in a Landscape: Essays in Antiquarianism* (Edinburgh: University of Edinburgh Press, 1976), 120.

33. Piggot, *Ruins in a Landscape*, 118.

34. See Ralph M. Williams, "The Publication of Dyer's *Ruins of Rome*," *Modern Philology* 44, no. 2 (1946): 97.

35. John Dyer, *The Ruins of Rome, Poems* (London: printed for R. Dodsley, 1761).

36. *The Beauties of British Antiquity; Selected from the Writings of Esteemed Antiquaries with Notes and Observations by John Collinson* (London: printed for the author, 1779), 8.

37. *The Beauties of British Antiquity*, vii.

38. On Keate, see Kathryn Gilbert Dapp, *George Keate, Esq., Eighteenth-Century English Gentleman* (Philadelphia: University of Pennsylvania Press, 1939).

39. Dapp, *George Keate*, 15.

40. George Keate, *Netley Abbey. An Elegy* (London: printed for J. Dodsley, 1769), 7.

41. Keate, *Netley Abbey*, 7, 13.

42. Janowitz, *England's Ruins*, 31.

43. *Critical Review*, 27 (1769), 154.

44. John Brown, *The Cure of Saul. A Sacred Ode* (London: printed for L. Davis and C. Reymers, 1763), 11.

45. Brown, *The Cure of Saul*, 12:

> Lo, *Hate* and *Envy*, sea-entomb'd,
> And *Rage* with Lust in Ruin sleep;
> And scoffing *Luxury* is doom'd
> To glut the vast and rav'nous Deep.

46. Thomas Warton, *The Pleasures of Melancholy* (London: printed for R. Dodsley, 1747), 5–6.

CHAPTER 6. THE FRAGMENTS OF MEMORY

1. See, for instance, Robert J. Griffin, *Wordsworth's Pope: A Study in Literary Historiography* (Cambridge: Cambridge University Press, 1995).

2. In recent years, scholars have reclaimed Smith from the relative obscurity into which she had fallen. See, especially, Jacqueline M. Labbe, *Charlotte Smith: Romanticism and the Culture of Gender* (Manchester: Manchester University Press, 2003) and Jacqueline M. Labbe, ed., *Charlotte Smith in British Romanticism* (London: Pickering and Chatto, 2008).

3. Stuart Curran, ed., "Advertisement to *Beachy Head*," *The Poems of Charlotte Smith* (New York: Oxford University Press, 1993), 215. All references to *Beachy Head* are taken from this edition.

4. "Advertisement to *Beachy Head*," 215.

5. John M. Anderson, "*Beachy Head*: The Romantic Fragment Poem as Mosaic," *Huntington Library Quarterly* 63, no. 4 (2000): 547.

6. David Mallet in his *Amyntor and Theodora* (1747) uses a similar technique of fragmentation by locating his tragic story on the fragmented Hebridean island of St. Kilda. In the "Preface" to his long-poem, he indicates the generic hybridity of his composition by noting that it was originally planned as a tragedy.

7. Oliver Elton, *Wordsworth* (London: Folcroft Press, 1969), 30.

8. See Mary Jacobus, *Tradition and Experiment in Wordsworth's* Lyrical Ballads (Oxford: Clarendon Press, 1976), and Stephen Parrish, *The Art of* Lyrical Ballads (Cambridge, Mass.: Harvard University Press, 1973).

9. The poem will be referred to by its abbreviated title of "Tintern Abbey" and will be cited from the following edition: Thomas Hutchinson, ed., *The Poetical Works of Wordsworth* (London: Oxford University Press, 1950).

10. See Schlüter, *Die englische Ode*, 180–83. See also, Sandro Jung, "Hymnal Elements in Wordsworth's 'Tintern Abbey'," *Miscelánea: A Journal of English and American Studies* 34, no. 1 (2006): 67–78.

11. Beth Lau, "Wordsworth and Current Memory Research," *SEL* 42, no. 4 (2002): 681. See also, Michael Vander Weele, "The Contest of Memory in 'Tintern Abbey'," *Nineteenth-Century Literature* 50, no. 1 (1995): 6–26.

12. D. F. Rauber, "The Fragment as a Romantic Form," *Modern Language Quarterly* 30 (1964): 212–21; 217.

13. Marjorie Levinson, *Wordsworth's Great Period Poems* (Cambridge: Cambridge University Press, 1986), 14.

14. Ibid., 14–15.

15. Ibid., 15.

16. Jacobus, *Tradition and Experiment in Wordsworth's* Lyrical Ballads, 48.

17. Ibid., 50.

18. S. T. Coleridge, *Biographia Literaria*, ed. George Watson (London: J. M. Dent, 1956), 48–49.

19. Levinson, *Wordsworth's Great Period Poems*, 15.

20. Ibid., 16.

21. Stuart Curran, *Poetic Form and British Romanticism* (New York: Oxford University Press, 1986), 76, 77.

22. Ibid.

23. Anne Janowitz, *England's Ruins: Poetic Purpose and the National Landscape* (Oxford: Blackwell, 1990), 7.

24. Ibid., 10.

25. Lau, "Wordsworth and Current Memory Research," 682.

26. Wolfgang Riehle, "The Fragment in English Romantic Poetry," *Classical Models in Literature*, ed. Zoran Konstantinovic, Warren Anderson, and Walter Dietze (Innsbruck: Institut für Sprachwissenschaft der Universität Innsbruck, 1979), 135.

27. Riehle, "The Fragment in English Romantic Poetry," 133.

EPILOGUE

1. Richard Terry, "Transitions and Digressions in the Eighteenth-Century Long Poem." *SEL* 32 (1992): 497.

2. Margaret Anne Doody, *The Daring Muse: Augustan Poetry Reconsidered* (Cambridge: Cambridge University Press, 1985), 64.

3. Ibid., 67.

4. Susan Stewart, "Scandals of the Ballad," *Representations* 32 (1990): 135.

5. K. K. Ruthven, *Faking Literature* (Cambridge: Cambridge University Press, 2001), 20.

6. Christine Gerrard, "Introduction," *A Companion to Eighteenth-Century Poetry*, ed. Christine Gerrard (Oxford: Blackwell, 2006), 2.

7. Gert Ueding, "Das Fragment als literarische Form der Utopie," *Etudes Germaniques* 41, no. 3 (1986): 351–62, 353: "[d]as [fragmentarische] Werk ist nicht mehr fertiges Resultat, das die Stadien seiner Entstehung in sich aufgehoben hat, sondern immer nur Zwischenstufe auf dem Durchgang zu einer größeren Annäherung an die nie erreichbare Idee der Vereinigung des mannigfaltig Getrennten."

8. Ueding, "Das Fragment als literarische Form der Utopie," 356.

Bibliography

PRIMARY TEXTS

Addison, Joseph. *The Spectator*, ed. Donald F. Bond. Oxford: Clarendon Press, 1965.

Akenside, Mark. *The Poetical Works of Mark Akenside*, ed. Robin Dix. Madison N.J.: Fairleigh Dickinson University Press, 1996.

Ash, John. *The New and Complete Dictionary of the English Language*. London: printed for Edward and Charles Dilly, 1775.

Bancks, John. *Miscellaneous Works, in verse and prose, of John Bancks. Adorned with sculptures and illustrated with notes*, 2 vols. London: printed by T. Aris, for the author, 1738.

Barnett, Mr. *Odes*. London: no printer, 1760.

The Beauties of British Antiquity; Selected from the Writings of Esteemed Antiquaries with Notes and Observations by John Collinson. London: printed for the author, 1779.

The Beauties of Sterne. Dublin: printed for W. Wilson, 1784.

Blair, Hugh. *Lectures on Rhetoric and Belles Lettres*. London: T. Cadell, 1785.

———. *A Critical Dissertation on the Poems of Ossian, the Son of Fingal*. London: printed for T. Beckett and P. A. De Hondt, 1763.

Boeoticorum Liber: or a New Art of Poetry. Containing the best Receipt for making all Sorts of Poems. According to the Modern Taste. Dublin, no date.

Brightland, John. *A Grammar of the English Tongue*. London, 1714.

Brooke, Charlotte. *Reliques of Irish Poetry*. Dublin: George Bonham, 1789.

Brown, John. *The Cure of Saul. A Sacred Ode*. London: printed for L. Davis and C. Reymers, 1763.

Buck, Samuel, and Nathaniel. "The South View of Halton Castle in the County of Chester" (c. 1720).

Burke, Edmund. *On the Sublime*. New York: P. F. Collier & Son, 1909.

Carter, Elizabeth, ed. *The Works of Epictetus, Consisting of His Discourses, in Four Books, Preserved by Arrian, 'The Enchiridion', and Fragments*, 2 vols. London: printed for F. C. and J. Rivington, 1807.

Chatterton, Thomas. *The Complete Works of Thomas Chatterton*, ed. Donald S. Taylor and Benjamin B. Hoover, 2 vols. Oxford: Clarendon Press, 1971.

———. *Thomas Chatterton: Selected Poems*, ed. Nick Groom. Cheltenham: Cyder Press, 2003.

Coleridge, S. T. *Biographia Literaria*, ed. George Watson. London: J. M. Dent, 1956.

―――. *Collected Letters of Samuel Taylor Coleridge*, ed. Leslie Earl Griggs, 6 vols. Oxford: Clarendon Press, 1959–71.

Cooper, Anthony Ashley, third earl of Shaftesbury. *Characteristics of Men, Manners, Opinions, Times*, ed. Lawrence E. Klein. Cambridge: Cambridge University Press, 1999.

Cowley, Abraham. *Poems*, ed. A. R. Waller. Cambridge: Cambridge University Press, 1905.

―――. *Abraham Cowley: Poetry and Prose*, ed. L. C. Martin. Oxford: Clarendon Press, 1949.

Croxall, Samuel. *An Original Canto of the Fairy Queen, design'd as part of his Fairy queen, but never printed. Now made publick, by Nestor Ironside, Esq*. London: printed for J. Roberts, 1714.

Cunningham, John. *An Elegy on a Pile of Ruins*. London: printed for H. Payne and W. Cropley, 1761.

Davenant, William, Sir. *Sir William Davenants's 'Gondibert'*, ed. David F. Gladish. Oxford: Clarendon Press, 1971.

Dennis, John. *The Grounds of Criticism in Poetry*. London: Geo. Strahan, 1704.

Dodsley, Robert. *The Art of Poetry*. London: R. Dodsley, 1741.

―――, ed., *A Collection of Poems in Six Volumes by Several Hands*. London: R. and J. Dodsley, 1763.

Dryden, John. *The Poems and Fables of John Dryden*, ed. James Kinsley. Oxford: Oxford University Press, 1961.

―――. "An Essay of Dramatic Poesy." *John Dryden: A Selection*, ed. Douglas Grant. Harmondsworth: Penguin, 1955.

Dyer, John. *The Ruins of Rome*, in *Poems*. London: printed for R. Dodsley, 1761.

―――. *"Grongar Hill" by John Dyer*, ed. Richard C. Boys. Baltimore: Johns Hopkins University Press, 1941.

Escapes of a Poetical Genius. London: Marshall Sheepey, 1752.

Fawkes, Francis, and William Woty, eds. *The Poetical Calendar. Containing a collection of scarce and valuable pieces of poetry*, 12 vols. London: printed by Dryden Leach, 1768.

Finch, Anne. *The Poems of Anne, Countess of Winchilsea*, ed. Myra Reynolds. Chicago: University of Chicago Press, 1903.

Gildon, Charles. *The Complete Art of Poetry*, 2 vols. London: Charles Rivington, 1718.

Gilpin, William. *Observations on the River Wye*, ed. Sutherland Lyall. Richmond: Richmond Publishing, 1973.

Glossographia Anglicana Nova, or, a Dictionary, interpreting such hard words of whatever language, as are at present used in the English Tongue, with their Etymologies, Definitions, etc. London: printed for D. Brown, 1719.

Gray, Thomas. *The Correspondence of Thomas Gray*, ed. Paget Toynbee and Leonard Whibley, 3 vols. Oxford: Clarendon Press, 1935.

Hamilton, William. *Poems on Several Occasions*. Edinburgh: printed for W. Gordon, 1760.

Hardyknute: A Fragment. Being the First Canto of an Epick Poem; With General Remarks and Notes. London: R. Dodsley, 1740.

Hughes, John. "Remarks on the *Fairy Queen*," *Eighteenth-Century Critical Essays*, ed. Scott Elledge, 2 vols. Ithaca: Cornell University Press, 1961.

Hurd, Richard. *Moral and Political Dialogues; with Letters on Chivalry and Romance*, 3 vols. London: printed for T. Cadell, 1788.

Jago, Richard. *Edge-Hill, A Poem*. London: J. Dodsley, 1767.

Jerningham, Edward. *The Magdalens: An Elegy*. London: printed for R. and J. Dodsley, 1763.

———. *The Nunnery. An Elegy*. London: printed for R. and J. Dodsley, 1763.

———. *An Elegy Written among the Ruins of an Abbey*. London: printed for J. Dodsley, 1765.

Johnson, Samuel. *A Dictionary of the English Language*. London: printed for J. and P. Knapton, 1755.

———. *The Lives of the Most Eminent English Poets; with Critical Observations on their Works*, ed. Roger Lonsdale, 4 vols. Oxford: Clarendon Press, 2006.

Keate, George. *Netley Abbey. An Elegy*. London: printed for J. Dodsley, 1769.

Keene, Elizabeth Carolina. *Miscellaneous Poems*. London: printed for Robert Dodsley, 1762.

Lady's Poetical Magazine. London: printed for Harrison, 1781.

Langhorne, John. *The Poetical Works of John Langhorne. In two volumes*. London: T. Beckett and P. A. de Hondt, 1766.

Lonsdale, Roger, ed. *The New Oxford Book of Eighteenth-Century Verse*. Oxford: Oxford University Press, 1984.

Lyttleton, George. *Poems, by the Right Honourable the late Lord Lyttleton*. Aberdeen: printed for, and sold by, J. Boyle, 1777.

Macpherson, James. *Fragments of Ancient Poetry*. Edinburgh: G. Hamilton and J. Balfour, 1760.

———. *The Poems of Ossian and Related Works*. Ed. Howard Gaskill, with an introduction by Fiona Stafford. Edinburgh: Edinburgh University Press, 1996.

Mallet, David. *The Excursion. In Two Books*. London: J. Walthoe, 1728.

The Museum, or, the Literary and Historical Register, 3 (1747), 480.

Ogilvie, John. *An Essay on the Lyric Poetry of the Ancients*, introduced by Wallace Jackson, Augustan Reprint Society Publication, No. 139. Los Angeles: Augustan Reprint Society, 1970.

———. "Essay on the Lyric Poetry of the Ancients." *Poems on Several Subjects*. London: R. Dodsley, 1762.

———. *Rona. A Poem: In Seven Books*. London: printed for John Murray, 1777.

Parnell, Thomas. *An Essay on the Different Stiles of Poetry*. Dublin: Edward Sandys, 1715.

Partridge, Eric, ed. *The Three Wartons: A Choice of Their Verse*. London: Scholartis Press, 1927.

Pemberton, Henry. *Observations on Poetry, Especially the Epic, Occasioned by the late Poem upon Leonidas*. London: H. Woodfall, 1738.

Penny, Anne. *Poems*. London: printed for the author, 1780.

Percy, Thomas. *Five Pieces of Runic Poetry, translated from the Icelandic language*. London: J. and R. Dodsley, 1763.

————. *Reliques of Ancient English Poetry, Collected by Thomas Percy, Bishop of Dromore*. London and Edinburgh: William P. Nimmo, 1881.

Poetical Dictionary, or, the Beauties of English Poets, 4 vols. London: Newbery, 1761.

Pope, Alexander. "Preface to the *Iliad*." *The Iliad of Homer*, ed. Maynard Mack, The Twickenham Edition of the Works of Alexander Pope. London: Methuen and New Haven: Yale University Press, 1967.

————. *Minor Poems*, ed. Norman Ault, The Twickenham Edition of the Works of Alexander Pope. London: Methuen and New Haven: Yale University Press, 1954.

Scott, James. *Odes on Several Subjects*. Cambridge: printed by J. Bentham, 1761.

Shenstone, William. *Select Works of William Shenstone*. Edinburgh: printed for T. Balfour and W. Creech, 1773.

Shepherd, Richard. *Odes Descriptive and Allegorical*. London: printed for M. Cooper, 1761.

Smith, Charlotte. *The Poems of Charlotte Smith*, ed. Stuart Curran. New York: Oxford University Press, 1993.

Spenser, Edmund. *Spenser: Poetical Works*, ed. J. C. Smith and Ernest de Sélincourt. Oxford: Oxford University Press, 1970.

Sterling, Joseph. *Poems*. London: printed for G. G. J. and J. Robinson, 1789.

Stockdale, Percival. *Lectures on the Truly Eminent Poets*, 2 vols. London: printed for the Author, 1807.

Thompson, William. *Poems on Several Occasions, to which is added Gondibert and Birtha, a tragedy*. Oxford: printed at the Theatre, 1757.

Thomson, James. *Winter: A Poem*. London: J. Millan, 1726.

————. "Liberty.' The Castle of Indolence,' and other poems, ed. James Sambrook (Oxford: Clarendon Press, 1986).

————. *The Seasons*, ed. James Sambrook (Oxford: Clarendon Press, 1981).

————. *The Seasons: Containing Spring, Summer, Autumn, Winter; by James Thomson: With His Last Corrections, Additions, and Improvements, with the life of the author: and An Essay on the Plan and Character of the Poem on The Seasons*. New York: Duyckinck, 1813.

Walpole, Horace. *The Letters of Horace Walpole, Fourth Earl of Orford*, ed. Paget Toynbee. Oxford: Clarendon Press, 1903.

Warton, Joseph. *Odes on Various Subjects*, ed. Richard Wendorf. Los Angeles: Augustan Reprint Society, 1979.

Warton, Thomas, ed. *The Union: or Select Scots and English Poems*. Edinburgh [actually printed in Oxford]: printed for the Author, 1753.

————. *The Pleasures of Melancholy*. London: printed for R. Dodsley, 1747.

————. *The Poetical Works of the Late Thomas Warton*, 2 vols. Oxford: at the University Press, 1802.

————. "Of Spenser's Stanza, Versification, and Language." *Observations on the Fairy*

Queen of Spenser. London: Robert and James Dodsley, 1762.

——. *The Oxford Sausage: or, Select Poetical Pieces*. London: printed for J. Fletcher, 1764.

Watts, Isaac. *Reliquiae Juveniles: Miscellaneous Thoughts in Verse and Prose*. London: Richard Ford, 1734.

Webb, Daniel. *Remarks on the Beauties of Poetry*. London: printed for R. and J. Dodsley, 1762.

Welsted, Leonard. *Epistles, Odes, etc. Written on Several Subjects with a Dissertation Concerning the Perfection of the English Language, the State of Poetry, etc*. London: J. Walthoe, 1725.

West, Gilbert, ed. *Odes of Pindar, with several other Pieces in Prose and Verse, translated from the Greek by Gilbert West*. London: printed for R. Dodsley, 1749.

Wood, Robert. *The Ruins of Palmyra, otherwise Tedmor in the desart*. London: printed for R. Dodsley, 1753.

Wordsworth, William. *William Wordsworth*, ed. Carlos Baker. New York: Holt, 1954.

——. *The Poetical Works of Wordsworth*, ed. Thomas Hutchinson. London: Oxford University Press, 1950.

Young, Edward. *Conjectures on Original Composition*. Leeds: Scolar Press, 1966.

——. *Night Thoughts*, ed. Stephen Cornford. Cambridge: Cambridge University Press, 1989.

——. *Ocean. An Ode: Occasion'd by His Majesty's late Royal Encouragement of the sea-service. To which is prefixed, an ode to the King: and a discourse on the ode*. London: printed for Tho. Worrall, 1728.

SECONDARY TEXTS

Anderson, John M. "*Beachy Head*: The Romantic Fragment Poem as Mosaic." *Huntington Library Quarterly* 63, no. 4 (2000): 547–74.

Backscheider, Paula R. *Eighteenth-Century Women Poets: Inventing Agency, Inventing Genre*. Baltimore: Johns Hopkins University Press, 2005.

Baines, Paul. *The House of Forgery in Eighteenth-Century Britain*. Aldershot: Ashgate, 1999.

Barrell, John, and Harriet Guest. "On the Use of Contradiction: Economics and Morality in the Eighteenth-Century Long Poem." *The New Eighteenth Century: Theory, Politics, English Literature*. Ed. Felicity Nussbaum and Laura Brown. New York: Methuen, 1987. 121–43.

Bate, Walter Jackson. *The Burden of the Past and the English Poet*. Cambridge, Mass.: Harvard University Press, 1970.

Beer, John. "Fragmentations and Ironies," *Questioning Romanticism*, ed. John Beer. Baltimore: Johns Hopkins University Press, 1995. 234–64.

Benedict, Barbara M. "Publishing and reading poetry." *The Cambridge Companion to Eighteenth-Century Poetry*, ed. John Sitter. Cambridge: Cambridge University Press, 2001.

———. "The 'Beauties' of Literature, 1750–1820: Tasteful Prose and Fine Rhyme for Private Consumption." *1660–1850: Ideas, Aesthetics, and Inquiries in the Early Modern Period* 1 (1994): 317–46.

Bowra, C. M. *From Virgil to Milton.* London: Macmillan, 1945.

Buxton, John. *The Grecian Taste: Literature in the Age of Neo-classicism, 1740–1820.* London: Macmillan, 1978.

Camion, Arlette, Wolfgang Drost, Geraldi Leroy, and Volker Roloff, eds. *Über das Fragment / Sur le Fragment.* Heidelberg: Carl Winter, 1999.

Chalker, John. *The English Georgic: A Study in the Development of a Form.* London: Routledge & Kegan Paul, 1969.

Christmas, William J. *The Lab'ring Muses: Work, Writing, and Social Order in English Plebeian Poetry, 1730–1830.* Newark: University of Delaware Press, 2001.

Cohen, Michael. "James Thomson and the Prescriptive Sublime." *The South Central Bulletin* 40, no. 4 (1980): 138–41.

Cohen, Ralph. "The Return to the Ode." *The Cambridge Companion to Eighteenth-Century Poetry*, ed. John Sitter. Cambridge: Cambridge University Press, 2001.

———. *The Art of Discrimination: Thomson's* The Seasons *and the Language of Criticism.* London: Routledge & Kegan Paul, 1964.

Cook, Patrick J. *Milton, Spenser and the Epic Tradition.* Aldershot: Ashgate, 1997.

Cory, H. E. *The Critics of Edmund Spenser.* Berkeley, Calif.: University of California Press, 1911.

Courthope, W. J. *A History of English Poetry.* London: Macmillan, 1905.

Curran, Stuart. *Poetic Form and British Romanticism.* New York: Oxford University Press, 1986.

Damrosch, Leo. "Pope's Epic: What Happened to Narrative?" *The Eighteenth Century: Theory and Interpretation* 29, no. 2 (1988): 189–207.

Dapp, Kathryn Gilbert. *George Keate, Esq., Eighteenth-Century English Gentleman.* Philadelphia: University of Pennsylvania doctoral dissertation, 1939.

Doody, Margaret Anne. *The Daring Muse: Augustan Poetry Reconsidered.* Cambridge: Cambridge University Press, 1985.

Dykstal, Timothy. "The Epic Reticence of Abraham Cowley." *SEL* 31, no. 1 (1991): 95–115.

Elias, Camelia. *The Fragment: Towards a History and Poetics of a Performative Genre.* Berne: Peter Lang, 2004.

Elton, Oliver. *Wordsworth.* London: Folcroft Press, 1969.

Erskine-Hill, Howard. *The Augustan Idea in English Literature.* London: Edward Arnold, 1983.

Finch, Casey. "Immediacy in the *Odes* of William Collins." *Eighteenth-Century Studies* 20 (1987): 275–95.

Fitzgerald, Robert P. "The Form of Christopher Smart's *Jubilate Agno.*" *SEL* 8, no. 3 (1968): 487–99.

Fowler, Alastair. *Kinds of Literature: An Introduction to the Theory of Genres and Modes.* Oxford: Clarendon Press, 1982.

Fromm, Waldemar. "Geheimnis der Entzweyung: Zur Ästhetik des Fragments in der Frühromantik." *Eurphorion* 94, no. 2 (2000): 125–47.

Fry, Paul H. *The Poet's Calling in the English Ode.* New Haven: Yale University Press, 1980.

Gedalof, Allan J. "Smart's Poetics in *Jubilato Agno.*" *English Studies in Canada* 5 (1979): 262–74.

Gerrard, Christine, ed. *A Companion to Eighteenth-Century Poetry.* Oxford: Blackwell, 2006.

———. *"The Castle of Indolence* and the Opposition to Walpole." *Review of English Studies* 41/161 (1990): 45–64.

Goldstein, Laurence. *Ruins and Empire: The Evolution of a Theme in Augustan and Romantic Literature.* Pittsburgh: University of Pittsburgh Press, 1977.

Griffin, Dustin. "Milton and the Decline of Epic in the Eighteenth Century." *New Literary History* 14 (1982): 143–54.

———. *Patriotism and Poetry in Eighteenth-Century Britain.* Cambridge: Cambridge University Press, 2002.

Groom, Nick. "Fragments, Reliques, and MSS: Chatterton and Percy." *Thomas Chatterton and Romantic Culture,* ed. Nick Groom. Basingstoke: Macmillan, 1999.

———. "Literature, 1757–1776." *A Companion to Literature from Milton to Blake,* ed. David Womersley. Oxford. Blackwell, 2000, 464–80.

Harries, Elizabeth Wanning. "'Excited Ideas': Fragments, Description, and the Sublime." *Del Frammento.* Ed. Rosa Maria Losito. Naples: Istituto Universitario Orientale, 2000, 30–47.

———. *The Unfinished Manner: Essays on the Fragment in the Later Eighteenth Century.* Charlottesville, Va.: University Press of Virginia, 1994.

Havens, Raymond Dexter. *The Influence of Milton on English Poetry.* New York: Russell and Russell, 1961.

Hunter, J. Paul. "Couplets and Conversation." *The Cambridge Companion to Eighteenth-Century Poetry,* ed. John Sitter. Cambridge: Cambridge University Press, 2001.

Irlam, Shaun. *Elations: The Poetics of Enthusiasm in Eighteenth-Century Britain.* Stanford, Calif.: Stanford University Press, 1999.

Jack, Ian. *Augustan Satire: Intention and Idiom in English Poetry, 1660–1750.* Oxford: Clarendon Press, 1952.

Jacobus, Mary. *Tradition and Experiment in Wordsworth's Lyrical Ballads.* Oxford: Clarendon Press, 1976.

Janowitz, Anne. *England's Ruins: Poetic Purpose and the National Landscape.* Oxford: Blackwell, 1990.

Johnston, Arthur. "Poetry and Criticism after 1740." *Dryden to Johnson,* ed. Roger Lonsdale, The Penguin History of Literature. Harmondsworth: Penguin, 1993. 313–49.

Jung, Sandro. "Form versus Manner: The Pindaric Ode and the 'Hymnal' Tradition in the Mid-Eighteenth Century." *Zeitschrift für Literaturwissenschaft und Linguistik*

144/36 (2006): 130–45.

———. "Some Notes on William Mason and His Use of the 'Hymnal' Ode." *Studia Neophilologica* 76, no. 2 (2004): 176–81.

———. "William Collins's 'Ode on the Poetical Character' and the 'cest of amplest power.'" *Neophilologus* 91, no. 2 (2007): 539–54.

———. "Updating *Summer*, or Revising and Recomposing *The Seasons*," in *On Second Thought: Updates in the Eighteenth Century*, ed. Elizabeth Kraft and Deborah Taylor Bourdeau. Newark: University of Delaware Press, 2007, 69–82.

———. "Epic, Ode, or Something New: The Blending of Genres in Thomson's *Spring*." *Papers on Language and Literature* 43, no. 2 (2007): 146–65.

Kaul, Suvir. *Poems of Nation, Anthems of Empire: English Verse in the Long Eighteenth Century*. Charlottesville, Va.: University Press of Virginia, 2000.

Keith, Jennifer. *Poetry and the Feminine: From Behn to Cowper*. Newark: University of Delaware Press, 2005.

Kenshur, Oscar. *Open Form and the Shape of Ideas: Literary Structures as Representations of Philosophical Concepts in the Seventeenth and Eighteenth Centuries*. Lewisburg: Bucknell University Press, 1986.

Kersey, Mel. "Ballads, Britishness and *Hardyknute*." *Scottish Studies Review* 5, no. 1 (2004): 40–56.

Kubiak, Christopher. "Sowing Chaos: Discontinuity and the Form of Autonomy in the Fragment Collections of the Early German Romantics." *Studies in Romanticism* 33, no. 3 (1994): 411–49.

Landry, Donna. *The Muses of Resistance: Laboring-class Women's Poetry in Britain, 1739–1796*. Cambridge: Cambridge University Press, 1990.

Larmour, Heather. "Anthologising the Author in the Eighteenth-Century 'Beauties' Tradition." Unpublished doctoral thesis, University of Liverpool, 2002.

Levinson, Marjorie. *The Romantic Fragment Poem: A Critique of a Form*. Chapel Hill: University of North Carolina Press, 1986.

———. *Wordsworth's Great Period Poems*. Cambridge: Cambridge University Press, 1986.

Lewalski, Barbara Kiefer. "The Genres of *Paradise Lost*," in *The Cambridge Companion to Milton*, ed. Dennis Danielson. Cambridge: Cambridge University Press, 1999.

———. Paradise Lost *and the Rhetoric of Literary Forms*. Princeton: Princeton University Press, 1985.

Lipking, Lawrence. "The Genie in the Lamp: M. H. Abrams and the Motives of Literary History." *High Romantic Argument: Essays for M. H. Abrams*, ed. Lawrence Lipking. Ithaca: Cornell University Press, 1981, 128–48.

Lucken, Christopher. "Ossian contre Aristote ou l'invention de l'epopee primitive." *Plaisir de l'epopee*. Ed. Giselle Mathieu-Castellani. Saint-Denis: Publications Universitaires de Vincennes, 2000, 229–55.

Mayo, Robert. "The Contemporaneity of the *Lyrical Ballads*." *PMLA* 69 (1954): 486–522.

McFarland, Thomas. *Romanticism and the Forms of Ruin: Wordsworth, Coleridge, and Modalities of Fragmentation*. Princeton: Princeton University Press, 1981.

McGann, Jerome. *The Textual Condition*. Princeton: Princeton University Press, 1991.

Miner, Earl. "From Narrative to 'Description' and 'Sense' in Eighteenth-Century Poetry." *SEL* 9, no. 3 (1969): 471–87.

Moore, Dafydd. *Enlightenment and Romance in James Macpherson's 'The Poems of Ossian': Myth, Genre and Cultural Change*. Aldershot: Ashgate, 2003.

Nochlin, Linda. *The Body in Pieces: The Fragment as a Metaphor of Modernity*. London: Thames and Hudson, 1994.

Ong, Walter J. *Orality and Literacy: The Technologizing of the Word*. London: Methuen, 1982.

Pala, Mauro. "Ruins of Awareness." *La Questione Romantica* 10 (2001): 83–94.

Parker, Blanford. *The Triumph of Augustan Poetics*. Cambridge: Cambridge University Press, 1998.

Patey, Douglas Lane. "Art and Integrity: Concepts of Self in Alexander Pope and Edward Young." *Modern Philology* 83, no. 4 (1986): 364–78.

Peake, Charles. "Poetry 1700–1740." *Dryden to Johnson*, ed. Roger Lonsdale, The Penguin History of Literature. Harmondsworth: Penguin, 1993.

Piggot, Stuart. *Ruins in a Landscape: Essays in Antiquarianism*. Edinburgh: University of Edinburgh Press, 1976.

Piper, William Bowman. *The Heroic Couplet*. Cleveland: Press of Case Western Reserve University, 1969.

Radcliffe, David Hill. *Edmund Spenser: A Reception History*. Columbia: Camden House, 1996.

Rajan, Balachandra. *The Form of the Unfinished: English Poetics from Spenser to Pound*. Princeton: Princeton University Press, 1985.

Rauber, D. F. "The Fragment as a Romantic Form." *Modern Language Quarterly* 30 (1964): 212–21.

Riehle, Wolfgang. "The Fragment in English Romantic Poetry." *Classical Models in Literature*, ed. Zoran Konstantinovic, Warren Anderson, and Walter Dietze. Innsbruck: Institut für Sprachwissenschaft der Universität Innsbruck, 1979, 133–38.

Rothstein, Eric. *Restoration and Eighteenth-Century Poetry, 1660–1780*. London: Routledge & Kegan Paul, 1981.

Ruthven, K. K. *Faking Literature*. Cambridge: Cambridge University Press, 2001.

Saintsbury, George. *The Peace of the Augustans: A Survey of Eighteenth-Century Literature as a Place of Rest and Refreshment*. London: G. Bell, 1916.

Sambrook, James. *James Thomson, 1700–1748: A Life*. Oxford: Clarendon Press, 1991.

Schlüter, Kurt. *Die Englische Ode: Studien zu ihrer Entwicklung unter Einfluß der antiken Hymne*. Bonn: Bouvier, 1964.

Sitter, John. *Literary Loneliness in Mid-Eighteenth-Century England*. Ithaca: Cornell University Press, 1982.

Smith, David Nichol. *Some Observations on Eighteenth-Century Poetry*. Toronto: University of Toronto Press, 1964.

Snead, Jennifer. "*Disjecta Membra Poetae*: The Aesthetics of the Fragment and Johnson's Biographical Practice in the *Lives of the English Poets*." *The Age of Johnson: A*

Scholarly Annual 15 (2004): 251–69.

Sportelli, Annamaria. "Sublimity and Fragmentariness: Forms and Discourse." *La Questione Romantica* 10 (2001): 49–60.

Stafford, Barbara. "'Illiterate Monuments': The Ruin as Dialect or Broken Classic." *The Age of Johnson* 1 (1987): 1–34.

Stafford, Fiona. *The Sublime Savage: A Study of James MacPherson and the Poems of Ossian.* Edinburgh: Edinburgh University Press, 1988.

Starr, G. Gabrielle. *Lyric Generations: Poetry and the Novel in the Long Eighteenth Century.* Baltimore: Johns Hopkins University Press, 2004.

Steinman, Lisa M. *Masters of Repetition: Poetry, Culture, and Work in Thomson, Wordsworth, Shelley, and Emerson.* Basingstoke: Macmillan, 1998.

Stewart, Susan. "Scandals of the Ballad." *Representations* 32 (1990): 134–56.

Strathman, Christopher A. *Romantic Poetry and the Fragmentary Imperative: Schlegel, Byron, Joyce, Blanchot.* New York: State University of New York Press, 2006.

Sühnel, Rudolf. "Tradition und Originalgenie: Bemerkungen zu Edward Youngs *Conjectures on Original Composition.*" *Geschichtlichkeit und Neuanfang im sprachlichen Kunstwerk: Studien zur englischen Philologie zu Ehren von Fritz W. Schulze*, ed. W. G. Müller and Peter Erlebach. Tübingen: Narr, 1981, 163–67.

Sutherland, James. *A Preface to Eighteenth-Century Poetry.* Oxford: Clarendon Press, 1948.

Teich, Nathanial. "The Ode in English Literary History: Transformations from the Mid-Eighteenth to the Early Nineteenth Century." *Papers on Language and Literature* 21 (1985): 88–108.

Terry, Richard. "Transitions and Digressions in the Eighteenth-Century Long Poem." *SEL* 32 (1992): 495–510.

Thomas, Sophie. "The Fragment." *Romanticism: An Oxford Guide*, ed. Nicholas Roe. Oxford: Oxford University Press, 2004.

Thomson, Derek S. "Macpherson's *Ossian*: Ballads to Epics." *Bealoideas: The Journal of the Folklore of Ireland Society* 54–55 (1986–87): 243–64

Tillyard, E. M. W. *English Epic and Its Background.* London: Chatto and Windus, 1954.

———. *The Epic Strain in the English Novel.* London: Chatto and Windus, 1958.

Treip, Mindele Anne. *Allegorical Poetics and the Epic: The Renaissance Tradition to Paradise Lost.* Lexington: University Press of Kentucky, 1994.

Ueding, Gert. "Das Fragment als literarische Form der Utopie." *Etudes Germaniques* 41, no. 3 (1986): 351–62.

Walker, Jeanne Murray. "*Jubilato Agno* as Psalm." *SEL* 20, no. 3 (1980): 449–59.

Walsh, Marcus. *Shakespeare, Milton and Eighteenth-Century Literary Editing.* Cambridge: Cambridge University Press, 1997.

Wasserman, Earl R. *Elizabethan Poetry in the Eighteenth Century*, Illinois Studies in English Language and Literature. Urbana: University of Illinois Press, 1947.

Weinbrot, Howard D. *Britannia's Issue: The Rise of British Literature from Dryden to Ossian.* Cambridge: Cambridge University Press, 1993.

Williams, Ralph M. *Poet, Painter and Parson: The Life of John Dyer.* New York: Bookman

Associates, 1956.

————. "The Publication of Dyer's *Ruins of Rome*." *Modern Philology* 44, no. 2 (1946): 97–101.

Wilson, Penelope. "'High Pindaricks upon stilts': A Case-Study in the Eighteenth-Century Classical Tradition." *Rediscovering Hellenism: The Hellenic Heritage and the English Imagination*, ed. G. W. Clarke and J. C. Eade. Cambridge: Cambridge University Press, 1989.

Index